The Vocation of Theology

THE VOCATION OF THEOLOGY

Inquiry, Dialogue, Adoration

Edited by
Rex D. Matthews

The Vocation of Theology: Inquiry, Dialogue, Adoration

The General Board of Higher Education and Ministry leads and serves The United Methodist Church in the recruitment, preparation, nurture, education, and support of Christian leaders—lay and clergy—for the work of making disciples of Jesus Christ for the transformation of the world. Its vision is that a new generation of Christian leaders will commit boldly to Jesus Christ and be characterized by intellectual excellence, moral integrity, spiritual courage, and holiness of heart and life. The General Board of Higher Education and Ministry of The United Methodist Church serves as an advocate for the intellectual life of the church. The Board's mission embodies the Wesleyan tradition of commitment to the education of laypersons and ordained persons by providing access to higher education for all persons.

Foundery Books is named for the abandoned foundery that early followers of John Wesley transformed into a church, which became the cradle of London's Methodist movement.

Contents

Foreword

Jan Love

As the dean of Emory University's Candler School of Theology, it is my privilege to say a few introductory words about the volume now before you. The chapters in this volume arose out of events that marked the centennial of the Candler School of Theology during the 2014–15 academic year. The essays are all written by Candler faculty members, who contributed their insights and expertise throughout the year under the theme "The Candler Centennial in Story and Prophecy," but particularly in two major events: a two-day fall commemoration that focused on story, memory and celebration; and a three-day spring academic conference that emphasized prophecy in the sense of speaking a word that challenged the world.

The fall commemoration took stock of our history over the last one hundred years. One of our aims was to recognize the breadth and depth of all those who brought us to this milestone and whose legacy will no doubt sustain Candler's vision in the century to come. Together we remembered, laughing and crying about the good times as well as the tender and tough times. In worship and other gatherings, we praised God for the faithful journey and remarkable accomplishments of faculty, staff, students, and alumni, often in the midst of seemingly insurmountable obstacles. We heard challenging tales of where we fell short in earlier eras and confessed that we did not always evince a faithful witness to the good news of Christ's love, grace, mercy, and justice. One of the small but important ways we sought to make amends was by hanging portraits of Candler's first tenured African American faculty member, Grant Shockley (1970–76 and 1989–91) and of the school's first tenured woman faculty member, Roberta Bondi (1978–2006). In all things, we gave thanks to God for the abundance of fruitful ministries of education, formation, and witness harvested across one hundred years.

Like any good story, Candler's history is best told through the actions of its heroes and heroines. We invited alumni, faculty, staff, and other members of the Emory University community to nominate candidates for a Centennial Medal, a special recognition for making extraordinary contributions to Candler, the church and the larger society. This group of notable women and men, including alumni, friends, faculty, staff, and administrators, is listed on Candler's website at htttp://candler.emory.edu/news/connection/centennial /feature-stories/centennial-medalists.html.They represent some of the best of Candler's story, whether their influence helped shape the institution of today, or they used what they learned to foster positive transformation in the world. Each person demonstrates one or more of the core commitments by which Candler defines itself: teaching and learning to transform Christian congregations and public life; scholarship to inspire the production of knowledge in critical and collegial conversation with the traditions of both church and academy; openness to honor the voice of every member of the Candler community across lines of confessional difference, disability, race and ethnicity, gender and generation, social and sexual identity, cultural heritage and national origin; dialogue to foster an intentionally diverse community of learning; and service to the world to form leaders dedicated to ministries of justice, righteousness, peace, and the flourishing of all creation.

Activities in spring semester 2015 sought to cast a vision for theological education in the twenty-first century. In March, we held an academic conference, "Prophetic Voices: Confronting Theological Challenges of the Next Century." We debated and discussed scholarly presentations by faculty and other scholars; we worshipped together and praised God; we prayed fervently as we sought to imagine anew how to be faithful witnesses to the gospel now and into the future; and we prepared ourselves for the task of speaking God's truth in our day and time as we continue to seek God's wisdom and guidance in fulfilling our mission of educating faithful and creative leaders for the churches' ministries throughout the world.

It is no accident that centennial events featured Candler faculty who are, as a whole, among the most prolific scholars at Emory University and in theological education. Moreover, they are deeply dedicated to teaching and serving the church and academy. The essays compiled in this book all stem from centennial events, but they are introduced with an additional essay from Dr. Don E. Saliers, a long-standing leader at the school and now Theologian-in-Residence. Some contributors have been at Candler for many years. Others are relative newcomers, but all are dedicated to the institution being "grounded in the Christian faith and shaped by the Wesleyan tradition of evangelical piety, ecumenical openness, and social concern," as our mission statement proclaims.

The vision cast by these faculty members arises in part from their context of research, teaching, and service at Candler, which may make this book a uniquely Candler contribution to theological education. Our hope is that scholars and leaders from elsewhere in the country and the world will critique, challenge, and widen our understanding of where God is leading us, an exercise that began during the spring academic conference.

Dr. Luke Timothy Johnson chaired Candler's Centennial Committee and guided the year-long commemoration. He conceived the theme of the centennial, "Story and Prophecy," and then in the wonderfully collegial Candler way, drew in the creative and collaborative work of numerous faculty and staff colleagues who put flesh on the bones of his original vision, bringing it to full life. He delivered the keynote address for the spring academic conference, which is included as chapter 7 in this volume. I am deeply grateful for his leadership and that of many others who made the year a success.

The spring academic conference was made possible by the generous financial support of the McDonald Agape Foundation, for which we remain very thankful. The generosity exhibited by the Honorable Alonzo L. McDonald and Mrs. Suzie McDonald and their family across many years has provided Candler with a number of opportunities to sponsor events that enliven, enrich, and deepen theological inquiry and discussion.

The centennial commemorations resulted in two books. The first was *Religion and Reason Joined: Candler at One Hundred* by Gary S. Hauk (Bookhouse Group, 2014); it chronicles the school's history across the century with engaging text and photos. The second is this one. Thanks are due to Dr. Rex D. Matthews, who employed his long-standing superb skills as a book editor to great effect in creating it. I am deeply grateful for his tireless dedication to the tasks of imagining and bringing to fruition this compilation of insightful and inspiring essays.

The cover art, *Festival of Lights,* is by Los Angeles artist John August Swanson. His works are found in the National Museum of American History in Washington, the Tate Gallery in London, the Collection of Modern Religious Art in the Vatican, and other public collections. The largest single selection of Swanson's work is displayed at Candler.

I hope the essays in this book will not only capture some of Candler's vision for and contributions to theological education, but will also stimulate vibrant discussions in other schools and among leaders in the church who care passionately about this crucial task that joins the church and the academy.

Acknowledgments

The art used on the front cover is *Festival of Lights* by John August Swanson, copyright © 2000 by John August Swanson. Serigraph, 30¾" x 24." Used by permission of the artist. For further information, see: http://www.johnaugustswanson.com.

All references to the writings of John Wesley unless otherwise noted are from *The Bicentennial Edition of the Works of John Wesley* (Nashville: Abingdon Press, 1984—) and are noted as *The Works of John Wesley*. Used by permission of the publisher.

An earlier version of chapter 8 was published as "From Silkworms to Songbirds: Why We No Longer Preach Like Jonathan Edwards," in *Commonweal*, vol. 42, no. 16 (October 9, 2015). Used by permission of the publisher.

The extract from the poem "Warrior's Dance (Tai Chi Chuan)" by Camilla Mac Bica (p. 117) is from the author's book *Worthy of Gratitude: Why Veterans May Not Want to be Thanked for Their Service in War* (New York: Gnosis Press, 2016), 26–27. Used by permission of the author.

The poem "Iraq" by Mary Oliver (p. 119) is from *Red Bird: Poems by Mary Oliver* (Boston: Beacon Press, 2008), copyright © 2008 by Mary Oliver. Used by permission of the Charlotte Sheedy Literary Agency, Inc.

The extract from the poem "Change Has Come" by Kelly Gissendaner (p. 121) is from an unpublished manuscript prepared during a creative writing course taught by Prof. Elizabeth Bounds at Lee Arrendale Prison, Georgia, in 2016. Used by permission of the author's estate.

The Vocation of Theology: Inquiry, Dialogue, Adoration

Don E. Saliers

What are Christian theologians called to teach and to write? Every generation asks this anew. There is, of course, a textbook answer: to interpret the faith and doctrine of the church and to relate the gospel to the contemporary world. This is the task of the Christian theologian. Yet, as the essays in this volume show, a textbook account hides the complex demands of such a vocation. From forty-two years of teaching at Candler School of Theology and Emory University, it is clear to me that the calling to theological work is not only to individuals; the calling is to collaborative communities of faith and learning. The three terms supplied in Carl Holladay's opening chapter and used in the title of this introductory essay and the volume—inquiry, dialogue, adoration—suggest that the work and idiom of theology is more like syncopated rhythm than a sustained chord or a simple melody, more akin to jazz and chamber music than to a solo recital. Yet, to keep the musical metaphor, there is also a *cantus firmus* that must be sounded in all modes of Christian theology: the glory and the mystery of God incarnate. Such a fundamental song-line must be sounded that God may be glorified in all things. This is no easy endeavor, since both lament and doxology are involved.

An unavoidable tension characterizes theological speech. God is beyond human conceiving, yet we address and reason together about the divine in human language. God is encountered in, with, and through the created world, human history, and in the patterns of human communal response. In short, God's relationship to the created world and to human beings is always mediated through the idioms of the world. This means that theological work must attend to all the domains in which the being and agency of God is active. The

1

essays in this volume move among those domains, advancing particular disciplinary engagements in the on-going work of one particular theological seminary marking its first hundred years.

Theology requires critical inquiry, dialogue and adoration. With a slightly different accent, Rowan Williams' three terms indicate a different order: celebratory, communicative and critical.[1] Theology springs forth from the worship of God, and from the struggle to live and to speak in the world accordingly. In other words Christian theology, like prayer and worship, begins by recognizing the gap between the world as it is and the world as it ought to be. Thus, one of the primary modes of theology is to offer, so far as possible, a full and compelling vision of God in relation to the whole of creation and the struggles of human history within it. But the travail of theology is then immediately evident. How shall such a vision be communicated? How shall a vision of God be expressed in ever-changing historical and cultural circumstances? Questions arise about what is to be preached, sung, prayed and taught. What shall we hope for? How shall we live in light of the story of God-with-us? How do we speak God-in-Christ in the midst of highly conflicted views of the world and changing conceptions of human ways of life? Theological work is intimately linked to the marketplace of human practices and the clash of viewpoints. This truth is present, sometimes quite explicitly, in each of the essays presented in this volume.

To ask about the "starting point" for theological reflection and communication leads back to something heard in several of the following theological voices. We may start with biblical exegesis, or with attention to ethical demands, global cultural diversity or with pastoral concerns; we may start with preaching and liturgy or with questions of what constitutes the church. But one starting point does not constitute the whole of theology. Luke Timothy Johnson's bold essay (chapter 7) proposes the risky task of theology as prophecy. There he sets forth four major topics that constitute a prophetic agenda for contemporary and future theological inquiry: theological

[1] Rowan Williams, *On Christian Theology* (Oxford: Blackwell Publishers, 2000), xiii.

imagination and secularization, the image of God in contemporary societies, care for creation, and the kingdom of God in light of global pluralism. These topics emerge out of Candler's commitment to free inquiry and passion for social justice. Addressing such issues requires an interrogation of the sources of theology in Scripture, church tradition, human reasoning and experience. Addressing these topics requires a reassessment of our understanding of the sources of theology, perhaps especially for us the Wesleyan traditions. For theology to be prophetic in the present time demands intense inquiry and dialogue coupled with a sense of humility.

Four essays take up the pressing topics directly. Ted Smith (chapter 8), Ellen Ott Marshall (chapter 9), Carol Newsom (chapter 11), and Jehu Hanciles (chapter 12) show how theology works. Woven together with the sermons of Tom Long (chapters 2 and 10), Brent Strawn (chapter 3), Luther Smith (chapter 4) and Teresa Fry Brown (chapter 13), we can also see how theological reasoning cannot be divorced from lively preaching. The Word of God proclaimed is also the interrogation of human history and the actual issues humanity faces. All of this is to say, the Christian faith has something crucial and critical to offer to world and to all churches.

Sooner or later, however, we find ourselves asking how theology finds common ground among the demanding questions and methods belonging to any starting point. The topics and the force of questions raised are characteristic of how theological work is done at Candler, or at any theological seminary worth its salt. To determine how a particular Christology, conception of the Trinity, or view of salvation and of human being bears on these concerns requires intentional interdisciplinary dispute and dialogue. This means diversity of voices listening carefully to each other. Such intentional critical dialogue is at the heart of theological education at Candler. This means, of course, that no one theological method or school will suffice. Yet all the specific inquiries that constitute a curriculum point to the question of how best to speak about God Incarnate in Jesus of Nazareth with integrity when faced with such a troubled and demanding world.

At Candler there is a clear accent on both practices and ideas and their mutual relationship. This has marked the vocation of theology for a century here, but with special intensity during the past fifty years. Carol Newsom has traced some of the history of these changes concerning women in chapter 5. This is a witness to the fact that theological speech and writing is always embodied and embedded in particular social cultural points of view. Theology, as we say, is "situated" in specific contexts of concern and thought. In the present time we have taught one another to mark and to appreciate *differences* in traditions and patterns of practice. Thus we sense the impact of gender, race, class, culture, and ideological elements in all of our sub-disciplines. If Christian theology is to have a form of truthfulness and integrity, we find ourselves faced with both a hermeneutics of appreciation, and a hermeneutics of suspicion. On the one hand how do we mark significant differences within Christian faith and the cultures in which it appears, while at the same time holding to the larger unity and promise of theological truth? On the one hand, we practice suspicion of any theology that claims "absolute truth" for itself; on the other hand, we return constantly to the desire to worship God "in spirit and in truth."

We might say, following the pattern in the book of Deuteronomy: "hear, remember, act" (where the act is also writing). This sensibility is worth cultivating. Theologians are called to listen for something, to look for something received in the rich memory of Israel and the church, something to which the texts point. At the same time, theology is called to discern the "signs of the times" in the present circumstances and the continuing gap between the "is" and the "ought to be" of our world. Without discerning the "signs of the times," the language of faith so easily remains self-enclosed, mute to the cries of the world and the travail of the churches. The "language of Zion" is more than conventional praise, it is a language of prophetic critique. To remember is to remember with a long tradition, taking the received texts and traditions to discern and interpret, and then to give verbal expression to the encounter of the traditions and the current circumstances of human life.

The richness of ecclesial traditions is a great blessing. We learn from one another across and sometimes even in spite of real differences. The classroom and the chapel are themselves akin to a gymnasium, as Tom Long reminds us in chapter 2. The impact of racial and gender diversity is nothing short of revolutionary, as these writers testify. Christian theology has nothing to fear from honest and truthful dialogue, even disputation resulting from this on-going history. It reflects what is always the case in the course of human life

4

in this world. Along the way, we uncover resources from past theologians we had not noticed. New questions reveal things we did not understand about the Christian tradition itself—about worship, about ethics, about moral imagination, about communities of justice and human compassion—about the divine participation. Following the rhythms of disciplined inquiry, sustained dialogue and an abiding sense of awe and worship set the conditions for expressing the Christian gospel—past, present, and future.

To form human persons in a way of life with these characteristics is a most worthy task. Doing theology in these modes makes demands on intellect, body and soul—and often strain our careful arrangements of order and power. But isn't that precisely the point of a theological vocation?

Each essay in its own way asks: What conversations have been fruitful? Which have avoided academic self-preoccupation? What conversations have yet to be engaged? Theological work requires qualities of attentiveness, rigor, and humility. To read the "signs of the times" without losing sight of the larger traditions to which the theologian is accountable—that is a hallmark of the integrity of Christian theology. The immense varieties of ways to address and be addressed by God found in Scripture are a clue to the practice of theology today.

Theology is not simply doctrines well dressed or defended, theology is a way of life. In my view, theology must trace all the implications of hope grounded in the very promises of God. The divine promises and the history of human witnesses to the hope of the world offered by Christian faith and life is the very stuff of our inquiry. Theological work is not incompatible with hard thinking, and prayer is fully compatible with critical reflection. A vision of life with God and neighbor is still the source and demand of our best work.

There is an old comic definition: a theologian is a thinker "whose premises are arbitrary but whose conclusions are irrelevant." As the following essays show, theological inquiry is alive; the dialogue is vigorous, and stretches out to acts of adoration. Our premises are grounded in real life, and our conclusions, though necessarily finite and tempered with humility, are grounded in the faithfulness of

God's messianic promises. Finally, the work of theology, born in a living encounter with the holiness and justice of God, leads back to worship. To praise the One whom we investigate and seek after—that passion is, as Kierkegaard observed, a "happy passion" which is deep faith. Only then can Christian theology supply discernment into the perennial human matters: what are we to hope for; what are we to live for; what are we to lament, what is praiseworthy?

That is the sense we can make of the claim that true theology begins and ends in praise of God.

CHAPTER 1

Imagining the Future

Carl R. Holladay

Fall Convocation Address
August 28, 2014
Text: Romans 12:9-21

T oday marks a moment of high celebration. On this day of every
academic year — Fall Convocation — we celebrate the arrival of a
new class of Candler students along with new faculty and staff, and
the return of other students, staff, and faculty. Today, however, this
communal re-gathering is enhanced by three other celebratory moments: the inauguration of Robert Franklin to the James T. and Berta
R. Laney Chair of Moral Leadership; the completion of the splendid
new home for Pitts Theology Library; and the beginning of Candler's
year-long centennial celebration.

Any one of these events would be ample reason to rejoice. So, today, in this single convocation event we are swimming in an ocean of
celebration.

Each of these celebrations is made possible through benefactions — *generous* benefactions that symbolize the enduring goodwill
of many good people. Student scholarships, named chairs, new
buildings, centennial celebrations all depend upon the generosity of
people committed to Candler's vision of a church galvanized by the
twin loves of God and neighbor and served by ministers summoned
and shaped by the gospel and trained in the best practices of faithful
Christian leadership.

As Asa Griggs Candler rightly observed in his famous "million
dollar letter," the generosity that establishes universities includes,
but extends well beyond, financial resources: "I fully appreciate,"
he wrote, "that one million dollars is insufficient to establish and
maintain the university which is needed for the church — indeed no

amount of money alone is adequate for such a purpose. The faith, the love, the zeal, and the prayers of good peoples must supply the force to do that which money without this cannot accomplish."[1]

While celebration is closely linked with benefaction, it also creates expectations. Students, new and old, come with expectations arising from calls born of newly imagined futures; but so do faculty, staff, and administrators whose sensibilities are shaped by our own sense of call and our respective visions of the future. Launching new chairs and building new buildings—such acts not only presuppose a future but they also boldly declare faith in the future.

From historians we have learned, not simply to search the past for lessons to be learned or examples to be emulated or avoided, but to reconstruct a usable past—a construal of the past critically understood—which is realistically grounded in what we know and do not know, or cannot know, about the past. We might also do well to think about the future in the same way—to develop, not naïve, utopian views of the future, but usable construals of the future that tread the fine line between apocalyptic pessimism, on the one hand, and rosy optimism on the other; to work with imagined futures that are predicated on an informed sense of what is possible, given what we know about the human capacity to deceive ourselves and God's capacity to surprise us.

Asa Candler's gift arose from a clearly articulated vision of the future. "In my opinion," he wrote, "the education which stretches and strengthens the mental faculties, without, at the same time, invigorating the moral powers and inspiring the religious life, is a curse rather than a blessing to [humanity], creating dangerous ambitions and arousing selfish passions. . . ."[2] This prosperous Atlanta businessman and devout Methodist layman could not imagine a viable future for society devoid of morally invigorating and religiously inspiring schools. For him, universities were places in which virtues could be cultivated and vices could be harnessed.

Asa Candler's letter is dated July 16, 1914—eighteen days after Archduke Franz Ferdinand, heir apparent to the Austro-Hungarian

---

[1] The letter, dated July 16, 1914 and addressed to his brother Warren A. Candler, has been widely reproduced. The original is in the collection of Asa Griggs Candler Papers (1821–1951), box 1, folder 9, Stuart A. Rose Manuscript, Archives, and Rare Book Library, Emory University.

[2] Ibid.

throne, and his wife Sophie, had been assassinated in Sarajevo, Serbia. On the same Thursday that Asa wrote his brother Warren, an ocean away, the *Times* in London was covering the heated debate on July 15 in the Lower House of the Hungarian Parliament about "the Sarajevo murders." Responding to tough questions, Prime Minister Tisza reassured the Parliament that "the present uncertainty" would require neither force nor the threat of force.[3]

But within three short weeks after this exchange in the Hungarian Parliament, unimaginable force was unleashed upon the European continent. Almost overnight, European visions of the future changed dramatically. Who could possibly have imagined a future in which the next five years would see the dissolution of three empires, the mobilization of 65 million troops, 20 million military and civilian deaths, and 21 million wounded?[4] The American diplomat and historian George Kennan called World War I "*the* great seminal catastrophe of [the twentieth] century,"[5] a sentiment echoed by countless historians.[6]

While 2014 is an important hundred-year marker for us, it is also a year of poignant remembrance for people the world over who live in places in which the embers from the Great War are still burning. As the political landscape of our own world changes with dizzying speed and patterns of global violence shift constantly, the July crisis of 1914 is a salutary reminder of how quickly—and how completely—our imagined futures can change.

It is often difficult to know how to speak of the future, a question frequently debated by ancient philosophers and theologians. Saint Augustine (appropriately quoted today, his Feast Day in Western

---

[3] Max Hastings, *Catastrophe: Europe Goes to War 1914* (London: William Collins, 2013), 49.

[4] Christopher Clark, *The Sleepwalkers: How Europe Went to War in 1914* (London: Penguin Books, 2013), xxi.

[5] George Kennan, *The Decline of Bismarck's European Order: Franco-Russian Relations, 1875–1890* (Princeton: Princeton University Press, 1979), 3.

[6] Clark, *Sleepwalkers*, claims that "the horrors of Europe's twentieth century were born of this catastrophe" (xxi), reiterating Fritz Stern's often cited thesis: "the first calamity of [the twentieth] century, the Great War, from which all other calamities sprang" ("Historians and the Great War: Private Experience and Public Explication," *The Yale Review* 82.1 [January, 1994]: 34–54, esp. p. 34).

Christianity), reflecting earlier debates in Plato, Aristotle, and Plotinus, devoted Book XI of *Confessions* to the topic of Time and Eternity, in which he quipped, "I know what time is until somebody asks me" (*Conf.* XI.xiv[17]).[7] These ancient thinkers recognized the categories past, present, and future as convenient fictions we use to organize our lives. Augustine observes, "The present considering the past is the memory, the present considering the present is immediate awareness, the present considering the future is expectation" (*Conf.* XI.xx[26]). Past and future are thus modes of the present. Of one thing Augustine was certain: Eternity is not simply an extension of Time into the indefinite future. "With God," he insists, "there is no then" (*Conf.* XI.xiii[15–16]; xxxi[41]).

The future may be elusive and events may unfold to shatter the futures we imagine, and yet, we still imagine the future—for ourselves as individuals, for our families, for the institutions of which we are a part—Candler, Emory, and the church. We choose our language carefully when speaking about the future. We speak confidently of shaping the future or embracing the future. We are less confident about predicting the future, which, as we all know, is a fool's errand, except perhaps for seasoned political pollsters like Nate Silver.

Our reluctance to predict the future is understandable. We are no longer confident that any future we can imagine, no matter how rosy, no matter how bleak, is unimaginable.

But our seemingly irrepressible human instinct to imagine the future resonates with the biblical narrative, which is pulled forward by imagined futures, beginning with God's promise to Abraham that all the families of the earth would be blessed through his descendants (Gen 12:3) and concluding with Revelation's final vision of a new heaven and a new earth—Paradise Restored—in which God's presence is fully experienced and where death and cries of pain are no more (Rev 21:1-4). Between these book-end visions of the future occur many other imagined futures of varying texture and scope. Sometimes they are prophetic, even utopian visions, imagining a return home to a devastated landscape but to the new possibilities that

---

[7] This quotation, and those following, are taken, with some modification, from Saint Augustine, *Confessions*, trans. Henry Chadwick, Oxford World's Classics (Oxford: Oxford University Press, 1998).

only freedom from slavery can bring. At other times they are more frighteningly apocalyptic, even militaristic and vengeful. They are typically crafted in artful metaphors that tease us and subvert our construals of the world, that challenge life as we know it, and the future as we imagine it. Thus Jesus proclaims that the kingdom of God is near—present in some sense yet still future. It is "among you," he says, and yet still not fully within our grasp.

Sometimes, as in today's epistolary text, we find moral visions— a future we might imagine, or even *must* imagine (the passage contains over two dozen imperatives)—for people who share a common faith: communities of faith in which love is genuine and in which mutual affection rather than pretentious self-interest orders our lives; in which service to the Lord is characterized by zeal and fervor, not reluctant, feet-dragging obedience; in which prayer and hospitality are deeply embedded, persistent practices that define the contours of our life together. Also envisioned are counter-cultural communities in which normal, even primitive, human instincts are reversed—blessing those who wish us ill or who would do us harm; repaying evil with good rather than multiplying evil in games of malevolent tit for tat; and reversing the downward spiral of vengeance by feeding our enemies rather than starving them.

Confronted with this variety of imagined futures, how do we find our way among them? How do we decide which ones to embrace or reject? And recognizing that our own imagined futures exhibit both constancy and change, how do we balance what should remain constant with what should change?

One place to begin is by reflecting on what the nineteenth century Austrian public lawyer Georg Jellinek called "the normative power of the factual," the notion that the *status quo* exercises a subtle persuasive power upon us, convincing us that the way things are is the way they should be.[8] If Jellinek is right, special discernment is required to identify where the kingdom of God has already broken in, then nurture that growth and sustain it; but at the same time to find those places where the seed of the gospel has not taken root and sprung up into new forms of life, and in those places actively aid and abet the birth of the kingdom of God. Only through

---

[8] Georg Jellinek, *System der subjektiven öffentlichen Rechte,* 2nd ed. (Tübingen: Mohr Siebeck, 1905); see Clark, *Sleepwalkers,* 361.

11

such careful discernment and active engagement can the way things are become the way they should be. Call it a form of prophetic discernment, with a strong dose of priestly, sagacious sensibility.

There are many ways to cultivate such gifts of discernment, but three formative elements—habits of the heart—can be singled out: a sense of *inquiry, dialogue,* and *adoration*. And that brings us to architecture and our newly completed buildings.

The powerful symbolism of Candler's newly configured space can scarcely be missed—a cluster of majestic buildings gracefully positioned on a slope, with classrooms, administrative and faculty offices in the Rita Anne Rollins Building at the base, Cannon Chapel at the crest, and Pitts Theology Library now firmly planted between them—all designed so that from Dickey Drive one enters spaces devoted to lectures, discussion, and administration, gradually ascending to space dedicated to reading, thinking, and writing, then moving even higher to a place of prayer, praise, and worship. Signs of intentional design are everywhere evident in this combined architecture that envisions a rhythm of life in which teaching, learning, administration, and worship flow together naturally rather than competing with each other as unnaturally aligned, competitive domains. One moves from classroom to library to chapel and back again in a natural, mutually reinforcing, pattern of formation.

Establishing a rhythm of life formed around the ancient ecclesial disciplines of *Quaestio, Disputatio,* and *Laudatio*—theological inquiry, discourse, and adoration—can yield a formational, pedagogical triad of interactive experience that gives our imagined futures, and the ways we live into them, a measure of realistic hope otherwise impossible. And so equipped, we can work together to change the way things are to the way things should be.

CHAPTER 2

God's Gymnasium

Thomas G. Long

Wesley Teaching Chapel Dedication Sermon
September 12, 2014
Text: 1 Timothy 4:7b-10

Today we are dedicating the beautiful Wesley Teaching Chapel in Candler's new building. Several years ago, when the first phase of our new building—what we now call the Rita Anne Rollins Building—had just opened, before construction on this building was even started, I was standing one day waiting on the elevator. I noticed a young man wandering haphazardly down the hallway looking vaguely lost. So I called out to him and asked if he needed any help. As it turned out, he was a prospective student exploring various seminaries, and he was making his first visit to campus to give Candler a look. So we struck up a conversation. He had a lot of questions about Candler—about the campus, the faculty, the curriculum and the kind of students who go here. At one point he asked me a bit of an odd question: "Is there a gym at Candler?"

I told him, "Well no, Candler does not have its own gym," but I assured him that if he came here he wouldn't be deprived because we do have access to the wonderful gym facilities over in the Woodruff Center. That seemed to satisfy him.

But I was thinking about that conversation and that question again as I was studying this passage in 1 Timothy. When Paul, the older minister, wants to encourage Timothy, the younger minister, in good ministry, he says, "Train yourself in godliness." The Greek word used here for "train" is *gumnaze,* from which of course we get the word "gymnasium." And when we get hold of what 1 Timothy actually means by training in godliness, I think it speaks provocatively to what we are doing today as we dedicate this chapel. I hope

13

that none of you will think it inelegant or inappropriate for me to suggest that this place, this beautiful place of learning and worship, is, in its own way, Candler's *gymnasium*.

See, what the author of 1 Timothy means by "training in godliness" is not going into a rose garden and being sweetly pious, but rather the hard work of practicing with one's whole being—body, heart, and mind—the Christian faith. Going to God's gym, if you will, and putting your whole body into the exercises.

One of the things that will happen here in this chapel is that our students will stand at this pulpit and preach—some of them for the very first time. It can be a wonderful and terrible moment for them, a crisis even, because this place is different from other places in this building. In other places in this building, they will turn in papers on theology and ethics and history and all the rest, and all to the good. But standing here, they will put their bodies, their whole lives, on the line in order that this gospel that comes out of their mouths is trustworthy and true. Here, they cannot hedge their bets. Because in this room, at this pulpit, they will be doing more than explaining the Christian faith; they will be confessing it, proclaiming it, bearing witness to it. This is Candler's gymnasium, where they will train in godliness.

Mary Donovan Turner, who teaches preaching at Pacific School of Religion, did her doctoral work here at Emory with Fred Craddock. In a book on preaching that she wrote with Mary Lin Hudson, a colleague in homiletics, she tells about a student who stood up in class to preach her first sermon. She had on the proper vestments; she had a neatly typed sermon manuscript on the pulpit; she had a carefully prepared sermon filled with sound theology and vivid illustrations; but when she opened her mouth to preach, her voice was a faint whisper. As Mary said, "She had something important to say, but she [literally] had no voice."[1] She had been schooled by her culture, trained by her family, indoctrinated by her church tradition that she had no authority to preach—no call to preach. What she needed, and what she got from Mary and her other seminary professors, was not shame, but encouragement and practice and exercises—what 1 Timothy would call "training in godliness"—that did far more

[1] Mary Donovan Turner and Mary Lin Hudson, *Saved from Silence: Finding Women's Voice in Preaching* (St. Louis: Lucas Park Books, 2014), xi.

14

than merely help her be an interesting speaker. They gave her her own voice to preach the gospel.

That's what we do here in the Wesley Teaching Chapel—in Candler's gymnasium.

The same is true for worship. It is one thing to know intellectually that the Table of the Lord is a place of God's hospitality, that people will stream from east and west, north and south, to gather at this feast. It's one thing to *know* that; it's another to let your body show that sense of welcome, to let your voice express the hospitality of Christ, as you preside at the table—to let your whole self announce the welcome of the grace of God.

Many years ago, when my stepsons were young teenagers, we took a family trip to Memphis. One of the places we visited was the National Civil Rights Museum, which is located in the old Lorraine Motel in Memphis. It was on the balcony of the Lorraine that Dr. Martin Luther King, Jr. was assassinated. One of the more striking exhibits in the museum is a bank of screens, some of them showing videos of civil rights workers in the 1960s receiving training in non-violence. There they are, sitting patiently at mock lunch counters, while other civil rights workers, playing the parts of antagonists and adversaries filled with hate, scream curses and insults at them and threaten them physically. Other screens show these same workers in real-life situations, sitting in at all-white lunch counters while people spit on them, revile them, and push them to the ground. All the while, they remain true to their training. They do not repay evil with evil, but respond with peace and non-violence, refusing to dehumanize their persecutors even as they are themselves being dehumanized.

They were able to do this because they had been to God's gym and had been trained in godliness. In here, we won't curse or revile our students, of course, but we will speak honestly to them. We won't simply say, "Beautiful worship," or "Fine sermon, pastor." We will speak the truth to them in love, because we want them to discipline themselves in ministry, to give their best in service to God and God's people.

That's what we do here in the Wesley Teaching Chapel—in Candler's gymnasium.

We will do this because ministry is not merely a set of ideas, but a vocation of embodiment, a vocation in which ministers are called to

15

put their bodies on the line, to show up with their whole selves in times of sorrow and times of joy. That is true from the very beginning of ministry all the way to the end. The powerful sign we share at the beginning of a ministry, after all, is not a beautiful thought or a disembodied act of the imagination, but the laying on of hands—the very physical and embodied act of the laying on of *hands.* Perhaps one day, someone will kneel in this very chapel, in this gymnasium where people are trained in godliness, and be ordained; and they will experience the laying on of hands.

In his autobiography, *With Head and Heart,* the preacher and theologian Howard Thurman describes how the memory of his own ordination could revive his commitment to ministry in times of struggle and doubt. When he was a young church worker, he decided that he wanted to be ordained as a minister, but he told his mentor in ministry that he did not want to have a laying on of hands as a part of the ritual. He wrote, "This custom was altogether too old-fashioned, I argued, with all the arrogance of youth." But his mentor, far wiser, balked, saying, "There will be the laying on of hands or there will be no ordination." And so there was.

Thurman writes,

> The ceremony of ordination was held at eight o'clock in the evening, and the moment of transcendent glory was for me the laying on of hands, which I had so strongly resisted. During the performance of this ancient and beautiful ritual "the heavens opened and the spirit descended like a dove." Ever since, when it seems that I am deserted by the Voice that called me forth, I know that if I can find my way back to that moment, the clouds will lift and the path before me will be once again clear and beckoning.[2]

Martin Copenhaver, who is now the president of Andover Newton Theological Seminary, describes his own ordination, and the laying on of hands, in equally powerful ways. As he knelt on the floor, people crowded around him. People placed their hands on his head until there was no room for any more. Then they placed hands on his shoulders, his arms, his back. Hands on top of hands, and he could feel the weight and the warmth of all of them. In fact, one hand

---

[2] Howard Thurman, *With Head and Heart: The Autobiography of Howard Thurman* (New York: Harcourt Brace, 1979), 57–58.

placed on him felt particularly heavy, and he wondered who *that* was. Was it his seminary mentor? His father? His wife? And then, in an instant, he knew: "That was Jesus' hand."[3]

Jesus' hand, placed heavily upon us, calling us to a ministry not simply of ideas, but a ministry of embodiment, a ministry where everything we are — minds, hearts, bodies — is trained to bear witness to the gospel. Ministry is this way because life is this way, too — embodied.

My father, who is in his nineties, took a fall in his assisted living facility last year and was taken by ambulance to the Emory University Hospital emergency room. Nothing was broken, thank goodness, but he was shaken and frightened by the experience. I took him to his physician for a follow-up examination, and the nurse had him put on a gown and sit on the examining table. Eventually, the doctor and two medical students entered the room. The doctor said to my father from the doorway, "So we've had a little fall, have we?" and then immediately turned to a computer screen in the corner of the room. He and the medical students conversed about the data flowing across the screen, and I couldn't help but think, "The data is on the screen, but the patient, the human being, is sitting, shivering, on the table over there across the room." Eventually the doctor and the students had decided all was well, and without a word they flew out of the room, their white lab coats flapping like seagulls on the wing.

The physician and Pulitzer prize-winning author Lewis Thomas wrote in his book about the practice of medicine, *The Youngest Science,* that young doctors are well-trained in medicine, but there are two important things they don't know. First, they have never been sick — not sick in a life-threatening way — and they do not know how it feels to be really sick. Second, they have been so schooled in tests and machines and data that they have forgotten that all healing begins with touch — with the willingness to place healing hands on the body of the one who is ill.[4]

Here in this place, we will train our students in godliness. We will

---

[3] Martin Copenhaver and Lillian Daniel, *This Odd and Wondrous Calling: The Public and Private Lives of Two Ministers* (Grand Rapids: Eerdmans, 2009), 138.

[4] Lewis Thomas, *The Youngest Science: Notes of a Medicine-Watcher,* Alfred P. Sloan Foundation Series (New York: Penguin Books, 1995).

ask them to put their bodies and their whole selves into the exercises done in this gym, so that when Jesus lays his hand on them and sends them forth to proclaim the gospel, they will put all that they have and all that they are into this holy work. And they will not hesitate to place the hand of blessing on those for whom and with whom they minister.

That's what we do here in the Wesley Teaching Chapel—in Candler's gymnasium.

CHAPTER 3

Congratulations!... Not So Fast!

Brent A. Strawn

Centennial Convocation Sermon
October 23, 2014
Text: 1 Chronicles 29:1-19

What does one say—what does one *preach*—at a centennial anniversary? That is a very good question and as I've stewed on it— for over a year now, since I was initially asked to preach at this occasion, and with the pressure of one hundred years of tradition bearing down on me—I've come to believe that there are actually *two* important things to say, two crucial things that must be preached at a moment like this one. Each of these things is found in the texts we have heard read and sung, but they are especially pronounced in the Old Testament lesson for this sermon, which comes from 1 Chronicles 29.

The First Thing to Say: Congratulations!

The first of the two things that should be said at a centennial anniversary like this one is related to the amazement one feels after hearing about David and the Israelites' work in 1 Chronicles 29. The text explicitly states that both David and the people rejoiced in this work (v. 9). And so, also, do we, when we witness a moment like that... and when we witness a moment like this one, right now. And so, as a result, the first thing that often comes out of our mouths at such moments—the first thing we say and that we probably should say at times like these is *congratulations*!

The situation in 1 Chronicles 29 is no less celebratory than our present one, after all, even though it is a good bit more fraught. David is on his way out, his son Solomon is on his way in; but "Junior" isn't yet up to the task of constructing the temple or gathering the

19

resources needed (v. 1). And the need is great. David needs help—a lot of help—and he gets it, in spades, or rather, in *kikkars*. And David leads by example: he kick starts the temple campaign with a lot of his own *kikkars* (3,000 of gold and 7,000 of silver). The king's treasure coupled with the overwhelming response of the people results in a spectacular pooling of finances: 8,000 *kikkars* and 10,000 *darics* of gold; 17,000 *kikkars* of silver; 18,000 *kikkars* of bronze; and 100,000 *kikkars* of iron.

Now, despite the fact that I'm an Old Testament professor, I have no idea what all of that means, but it sure sounds impressive, doesn't it? I mean, that's a lot of *kikkars*! 153,000 to be precise (including those *darics*). And, I'm just kidding, of course: I do know a little about what all those *kikkars* mean. For one thing, it's almost five thousand tons of material. For another, according to some scholars, a *kikkar* (sometimes translated as a "talent") is equivalent to 6,000 *denarii* and a *denarius* was one day of work. So, 153,000 *kikkars* would be the monetary equivalent of 918,000,000 days of work. Now that really *is* impressive. It's also about twenty-five thousand times longer than Candler's celebration of one hundred years (which would be only 36,500 days, not counting leap years). No wonder Israel and David rejoiced. No wonder we feel like congratulations are in order for David and Israel for this overwhelming, wholehearted support of God's work (v. 9).

But congratulations are also in order, now, here, for Candler. One hundred years may only be about six *kikkars* in terms of days worked, but that isn't too shabby. Neither is what the school has accomplished during that century. You have perhaps dipped into the recent history of Candler that was written by Gary Hauk, as have I, and have been both pleased and impressed to learn of all that is included in the school's history.[1] And I should make a quick correction to my math: six *kikkars* would be *only one person's* toil for one hundred years. Thankfully, Candler—no less than ancient Israel—has had more than one person toiling in these fields. Hundreds of faculty and staff, thousands of students and alumni have contributed, if not a full *kikkar* (16.4 years), then at least countless *denarii* to the Candler cause. And when you add all those folk in, along with all

---

[1] Gary S. Hauk, *Religion and Reason Joined: Candler at One Hundred* (Covington, GA: Bookhouse Group, 2014).

their days and years of labor—well, the *kikkar* ticker starts running up fast. So, here at Candler, today, in this moment, no less than in Chronicles, back then, in that moment, there is much to be amazed at, a lot to congratulate each other about, a great deal to be thankful for, bringing to mind the words of Psalm 124:1,

> If the LORD hadn't been on our side—let Israel now say!—
> if the LORD hadn't been on our side—let Candler now repeat![2]

Well, I added that last little bit, but you get the point of the psalm. If it hadn't been the Lord . . . well, then, when we were attacked, we would have been defeated; when the floods came, we would have been drowned. But we weren't destroyed; we didn't drown. We escaped, says the psalmist, because "our help is in the name of the LORD, the maker of heaven and earth"(Ps 124:8).

Yes, there is much to be thankful for, to be amazed at, to say *congratulations* about. Just think of all that has happened at Emory over the past one hundred years and the Candler School of Theology is still standing. We've weathered a lot of storms, outlasted whole other departments, units, schools! It's stunning to think about all that, to realize that there is no other top twenty-five, Research I university in the world that has a denominationally-affiliated school of theology on its campus and that cares as deeply and profoundly about religion as does Emory. And Emory is that way in no small measure because of Candler and all the people of Candler, working, for over one hundred years, offering all those *kikkars*. When you think about all that, it's truly remarkable. Overwhelming even. It makes us want to say *congratulations*! And we should say congratulations because that's the first thing that should be said at a centennial celebration like this one.

The Second Thing to Say: Not So Fast!

But there is a second thing to say at a centennial celebration like this one and it follows hard on the heels of *congratulations*! It is simply this: *not so fast!* Psalm 124:1 already gets at the point, doesn't it?

> If *the* LORD hadn't been on our side—let Israel now say!—
> if *the* LORD hadn't been on our side—let Candler now repeat!

---

[2] NIV altered. Unless otherwise noted, as here, all Scripture quotations in this chapter are from the CEB translation.

21

Did you hear it? If *the Lord. . . . Congratulations?* Well, maybe. But to whom are the congratulations due?

In 1 Chronicles 29, David knows about this second thing that should be said, this *not so fast.* He has given extensively and generously from his own private treasure (v. 3). And the rest of the people—let's call them the Temple donors, the Temple's "Committee of 100"—they've matched his gift in spades/*kikkars*, outgiving him in fact, and everything ends up in great joy "because they had presented their offerings to the LORD so willingly and wholeheartedly." And things could have ended right there, might have stopped right there, with *congratulations*—with *self-*congratulations.

But they don't stop there because David knows the truth of Psalm 124 (which is, by the way, a Davidic psalm). David knows "if *the LORD* hadn't been on our side. . . ." And so, in 1 Chronicles 29, after setting an example and summoning the people to respond, he doesn't stop with *congratulations*—and certainly not with congratulations *to himself or to the people.* Instead, he takes a deep breath and blesses God before the whole assembly (v. 10a), which is to say he offers a prayer to the Lord.

David's prayer is, as we would expect at such an occasion, both substantive and profound. "Blessed are you, LORD . . . forever and always" (v. 10b). "To you, LORD," he continues, belongs everything: "greatness and power, honor, splendor, and majesty"(v. 11a)—absolutely everything because "everything in heaven and on earth belongs to you"(v. 11b). And so, David says, or rather *prays*, God is king, ruler, head of all; the source of wealth, and honor; the one who has strength, might, and the power to magnify and strengthen everyone and everything (vv. 11-12). So "now, our God," he sums up, "we thank you and praise your glorious name"(v. 13).

But David's prayer is not yet finished because if all of that is true— or, rather, *because* all of that *is* true—something else must be said. "Who am I," David asks, "and who are my people, that we should be able to offer so willingly? Since everything comes from you, we have [only] given you that which comes from your [very] own hand"(v. 14; CEB altered). Did you catch that? All the *kikkars* are impressive, sure; and the people's overwhelming response is truly a cause for joy; David's exemplary leadership indubitably marvelous. But none of that is cause for congratulations—at least not to David and not to Israel. All the *kikkars*, all the giving, even the very willingness to give

22

in the first place—it all comes from God. It all "comes from your hand," David prays, "and belongs to you"(v. 16). "If the LORD hadn't been on our side, let Israel now say! *The LORD*, let Candler now repeat!"

This part of David's prayer makes a stunning theological claim—a claim that reorients our congratulations at profound moments like this one, a claim that rebukes any and all our temptations to *self*-congratulations. And we have to admit, don't we, that we are often tempted to *self*-congratulations? Our centennial, after all—*our* centennial—is profound! It is one of "story and prophecy"! And one hundred years of both! We've outlasted other departments, units, whole schools at Emory! We have a story! We are prophetic (or so we'd like to think)! *Congratulations* are in order! But *not so fast*!

Listen to David again: "Who are we, O God? And who are our people, that we should be able to give you so willingly all these *kikkars*, all these years, all this work? Everything comes from you— what we've given is only what has come from your own hand in the first place."

And hear the psalmist one more time: "If the LORD hadn't been on our side, let Israel now say, let Candler now repeat."

Congratulations may be the first thing one needs to say at a time like this, yes, but it is not the only thing. The second thing that needs to be said at a time like this is *not so fast*. Whom do we think we are congratulating? We might need to think again about that.

Now and (for) the Future

Since I'm meddling, bear with me as I meddle a bit more. Yes, we have much in our one hundred years to be proud of, to be thankful for, to say *congratulations* about. But Candler at one hundred, like Israel and David, knows it hasn't always been a highlight film. The offering of our *kikkars* hasn't always been wholehearted or willing. Sometimes the *kikkars* haven't been given to God at all, but retained, restrained, hoarded. Our school, no less than our larger university—no less than the people of God in Scripture—has been plagued by Sin with a capital S, and scarred by too many lower-cased sins to recount: systemic and individual; institutional, societal, and personal. David is right: I mean, really, who are *we* that we should be able to offer so willingly to God and God's work? Especially when we have to admit that sometimes we haven't offered *at all*, let alone *willingly*.

23

David knows all this full well. And so, in 1 Chronicles 29, he ends his prayer by praying about the future. "LORD, God of our ancestors . . . keep these thoughts in the mind of your people forever, and direct their hearts toward you," he says (v. 18). Don't let the people forget this wholehearted willing devotion, this perfect obedience. Fix it in their brains, in their hearts, so that they are kept on the right path, pointed in the right direction, toward you. And don't forget Solomon, David is quick to add. "Give him the wholehearted devotion [he needs] to keep your commands, laws, and regulations—observing all of them— and [the devotion he needs] to build the temple"(v. 19, CEB altered).

This kind of prayer for the future, for future generations—for God's help with all that—is absolutely necessary, given the pockmarked history of Israel. Of Candler. And that kind of prayer is not only necessary, it can prove highly effective. If God is all that David prays God is—if God is the source of all, even of our best, more generous obedience—then God is certainly able to answer this prayer, certainly powerful enough to keep these thoughts in our minds forever, certainly capable of directing our hearts toward the Lord (v. 18). And not just our hearts, but also those who come after us—our next generation.

Psalm 127, just a couple psalms away from Psalm 124, is attributed to the son David prayed for, his next generation: Solomon, the Temple builder. It begins this way: "Unless it is the LORD who builds the house, the builders' work is pointless"(v. 1). As you probably know, the Hebrew word for "house"is the same one typically used for the Temple. Unless the LORD builds the Temple, Solomon's psalm says, the work is pointless. Solomon, it seems, learned David's prayer in 1 Chronicles 29 by heart. The Lord may need *kikkars*, may need people who offer them willingly and wholeheartedly, but even then, in the best case scenario, it isn't *their* house. It isn't *their* achievement, *their* celebration, *their* centennial. If it is, then it's all pointless, meaningless, something that won't even make a ripple in the grand sweep of things, even if lasts one hundred years—even if it lasts longer.

I realize that's a bit of a harsh word, especially on this morning, in this centennial celebration. On this morning, in this moment, we want to claim the best bits of Psalm 127 for ourselves and for Candler: claiming that it is the Lord who has been at work building this house, and here it stands, one hundred years later, and so our work is not, and hasn't been, pointless. Of course we want to say that, especially at our centennial! And it *is* true. The Lord has built this house through the gifts and graces and the blood, sweat, and tears of hundreds of faculty and staff, thousands of students, millions of hours of reading, writing, lecturing, preaching, teaching, talking, kvetching, and meetings—the bazillions of meetings, the bazillions and bazillions of *faculty* meetings. And here the house stands, one hundred years later. Thanks be to God for building this house.

But like so many words of Scripture, there is another side to its two-edged blade—the one that cuts us, not just our foes. Unless the Lord builds the house, the psalmist says, the builders work for naught. And we have to admit—maybe not on this day, certainly not on this day, but alas, yes, even on this day—that not all of our work on this house has been the Lord's work. Much, then, has been pointless.

And then we really start feeling like David, don't we? Who am I and who are we, to stand here trying to give God what is already God's, especially when we have to admit that we often don't give it at all, don't even try to give it, that we've been doing it ourselves, all by ourselves, all for ourselves, pointlessly. *Congratulations . . . not so fast* may, in the end, be far too generous. How about *congratulations not at all*? That may be more accurate.

But even that—even that is a gift. Realizing that. Let me explain: David's prayer in 1 Chronicles 29 for his people and for his son—his prayer about the human incapacity to give God anything that is not already God's—that prayer no less than all the *kikkars* is a gift *to* God and a gift *from* God since it is God who enables gifts and gift-giving in the first place.[3] David's prayer that recognizes his lack of worth, his impermanence, his insignificance (v. 15)—David's prayer that begs God to keep God's people close, that implores God to keep his son Solomon even closer (vv. 18-19)—all of that, too, somehow, someway is also God's own gift, made possible by the One to whom everything and everyone in heaven and on earth belongs (v. 11).

Hearing *not so fast* after the *congratulations* isn't just a harsh word, then, a persnickety attempt to somehow rain on Candler's hundred-year parade. No. It's a gift. It's a reminder to us, to this university, to

---

[3] See the comments by J. Gerald Janzen, *When Prayer Takes Place: Forays into a Biblical* World, ed. Brent A. Strawn and Patrick D. Miller (Eugene, OR: Cascade Books, 2012), 343–44.

25

the whole world that "by ordinary human standards" not many of us were "wise . . . [or] powerful . . . [or] from the upper class"when we were called (1 Cor 1:26, CEB altered). "But God chose what the world considers foolish to shame the wise," Paul writes in 1 Corinthians. "God chose what the world considers weak to shame the strong. . . . God chose what [is] low-class and low-life—what is thought to be nothing—to reduce what is considered to be something to nothing. *So that no human being might brag in the presence of God . . . as it is written 'The one who brags should brag in the Lord!'*" (1 Cor 1:27-29; CEB altered).

And that brings to mind one last psalm, Psalm 115, which is not attributed to David or Solomon, nor to anyone else for that matter. I'd like to think that means that it might be attributed to us here and now, on this auspicious day, in this celebratory moment, at the centennial of the Candler School of Theology. Here it is:

> Not to us, LORD, not to us—
> > no, but to your own name give glory
> > because of your loyal love and faithfulness!
> Why do the nations say, "Where's their God now?"
> Our God is in heaven—he can do whatever he wants!
> . . . .
> [Y]ou, Israel, [Candler] trust in the LORD!
> > God is [our] help and shield.
> Trust in the LORD, house of Aaron [house of Candler]!
> > God is [our] help and shield.
> You who honor the LORD, trust in the LORD!
> > God is [our] help and shield.
> . . . .
> May the LORD add to [our] numbers—
> > both [us] and [our] children.
> May [we] be blessed by the LORD,
> > the maker of heaven and earth!
> . . . .
> [And] We will bless the LORD
> > from now until forever from now!
> Praise the LORD! (Ps 115:1-3, 9-11, 14-15, 18; CEB altered)

"Praise the LORD!" That's another way of saying *congratulations.* Just not to us.

Amen.

CHAPTER 4

Since We Are Surrounded

Luther E. Smith Jr.

Centennial Convocation Sermon
October 24, 2014
Text: Hebrews 11:32–12:2

We are surrounded by so great a cloud of witnesses! Do you see them? This room is crowded beyond what the fire marshals allow. And if you do not see them, do you feel their presence? Some we have known personally as faculty, staff, students, donors, church members, friends, and family. We could call their names, but if we started to call their names now, this convocation service would go days beyond the noon hour. So we silently remember them with affection and gratitude.

And there are witnesses we have discussed in Candler's classrooms: Martin Luther and Martin Luther King Jr., Son Yang-Won, Dorothy Day, Dietrich Bonhoeffer, the apostle Paul, John Wesley, Teresa of Avila, Sojourner Truth, Jeremiah, Mary, Howard Thurman and . . . and . . . and. . . . They are not sitting in sections according to our curriculum; for some reason, they refuse to be segregated and confined that way.

We do not know the names of the greatest number who surround us. We do not know their stories of faithful witness. Still, they are here surrounding us. Why are they here? All Saints' Day is not until next week. What do they want us to know about them? What are they longing for us to become and do?

Chapter 11 of Hebrews begins by characterizing faith as "the assurance of things hoped for, the conviction of things not seen." I like the way New Testament scholar Clarence Jordan interprets this verse. In his *Cotton Patch Version of Hebrews and the General Epistles,* he writes, "Now faith is the turning of dreams into deeds; it is betting

27

your life on the unseen realities."[1] Jordan's version is clear that "conviction" is more than intellectual consent to a set of doctrines or religious principles. Conviction means giving your life to unseen realities. It's being "all in" to pursue what God is pursuing.

The writer of Hebrews instructs on the meaning of faith by pointing to the lives of the witnesses. By faith Abel offered to God a more acceptable sacrifice. By faith Enoch was taken so that he did not experience death. By faith Noah respected God's warning. By faith Abraham . . . by faith Isaac . . . by faith Jacob . . . by faith Joseph . . . by faith Moses . . . by faith Rahab. . . . The writer then switches to the phrase "through faith" to refer to the countless number of persons who submitted their lives to God in service, battle, prophecy, and martyrdom.

For one hundred years Candler has been a place to learn about the cloud of witnesses and how the witnesses are our teachers about faith for the present and future. These witnesses have so much to show us and tell us and to demand of us. G. K. Chesterton argued the importance of tradition to understanding faith when he wrote:

> Tradition means giving votes to the most obscure of all classes, our ancestors. It is the democracy of the dead. Tradition refuses to submit to the small and arrogant oligarchy of those who merely happen to be walking about . . . tradition objects to [the ancestors] being disqualified by the accident of death.[2]

I believe that Chesterton is right. The ancestors get a vote.

In addition to Candler as a place to learn about the witnesses, *Candler has been a place for the formation of witnesses. And Candler has been a place of witness.* Over these one hundred years, vocations to "live by faith" have come to Candler, have been nurtured by Candler, and have been encouraged by Candler to serve God's passion for the world.

- By faith, many students have left successful careers and secure jobs to come to Candler to pursue a theological education

---

[1] Clarence Jordan, *The Cotton Patch Version of Hebrews and the General Epistles* (New York: Association Press, 1973), 35.

[2] G. K. Chesterton, "Orthodoxy," in *The Chesterton Reader: 21 Works in One Volume (Unexpurgated Edition),* (Halcyon Press, 2009), Kindle edition, location 7314.

even when there were no assurances of scholarships or being welcomed by the church.

- By faith, students have allowed themselves to experience the grief of relinquishing their treasured biblical and theological interpretations because they realized how inadequate their interpretations were to follow Jesus, "the pioneer and perfecter of our faith" (Heb 12:2).

- By faith, international students have left their homelands and families to come to Candler despite their disorienting experiences of alienation and estrangement.

- By faith, staff have not only gone the second-mile in accomplishing work for Candler, they have often attended to the bruised hearts in the community.

- By faith, custodians, making their rounds cleaning and discarding trash from our spaces, have spoken words of encouragement to students, staff, and faculty.

- By faith, Candler has changed policies and practices that prevented gender and racial diversity in its faculty and student body.

- By faith, many faculty have cared for students who were hungry, homeless, emotionally troubled and spiritually adrift even though such responsibilities were not in their job descriptions.

- By faith, the faculty have participated in ministry reflection seminars with students despite the fact that they (the faculty) were often bewildered and unsettled by the places where students served.

- By faith, Candler deans and faculty have defended academic freedom even when outcries and murmurings of heresy persisted.

- By faith, Candler graduates have given pastoral counsel as chaplains in the midst of the traumas of war, homelessness, incarceration, sickness, and death.

- By faith, Candler graduates have challenged the prejudices in their churches and the injustices in their communities even though many were forced to go elsewhere because of their witness.

- By faith, Candler graduates have served congregations, sometimes with twenty members and sometimes with thousands of members, with a whole-hearted commitment to care for their people's spiritual growth.

- By faith, persons of considerable financial means and those with only "the poor widow's mite" have contributed to support the education of Candler students.

What a wonderful tradition of witness . . . by faith! I repeat, Candler has been *a place for the formation of witnesses.* And Candler has been *a place of faithful witness.*

In its hundred-year history, Candler has also been slow to correct realities of prejudice, discrimination, and injustice that have been exhibited in Candler's own life—realities that caused emotional debates among faculty and among students. Debates that involved frustration, anger, and tears. Long periods of wondering if the school would be faithful to its public pronouncements about the necessity to become the diverse community God calls us to be.

Many of the achievements we celebrate in this centennial year are also a confession about our history of inaction. This celebration would be dishonest and pretentious if we did not acknowledge our need to confess. Confession, as in the liturgy of a worship service, is fundamental to celebrating the privilege of being in the presence of God and to offering ourselves to God's call upon us. All of us live imperfect lives; yet we are still the people that God calls to bear witness to faith. Our imperfections have not disqualified us as witnesses. Look to the cloud of witnesses that surrounds us, and you will not find a perfect life. Each witness has made choices that require confession. If perfection is the criterion for companions on your faith journey, prepare to be lonely.

Confession liberates us from the spirit-breaking weight of carrying our mistakes. By faith, we confess. By faith, we confess our fears. By faith, we confess our inaction. By faith, we confess our guardianship of the status quo. By faith, we confess that the significance of our projects often has narrowed our attention to the point of not seeing the suffering all around us—suffering that God urges us to see. By faith, we confess that some students needed and deserved more counsel from us. By faith, we confess that many of us have uncertainties about worship being essential to our educational mission. By faith, we confess that we sometimes doubt our ability to fulfill our mission. By faith, we confess that we too often forget what it means to keep Sabbath in this place. By faith, we trust that God will hear our confession and *free us* from any guilt or pride or indifference that prevents us from running "with perseverance the race that is set before us."

What a privilege it is to be free "to run with perseverance the race that is set before us, looking to Jesus the pioneer and perfecter of our faith" (Heb 12:1-2). What a privilege, and what an awesome responsibility!

When I read Candler's statements about its mission, commitments, vision, and core values,[3] I perceive that we are not only looking to tradition and the ancestors that surround us, we are looking to Jesus whose life embodied the very meanings of faith for loving God and loving neighbor. We endeavor to establish a theological school that prepares leaders who will give themselves fully to what is revealed through Jesus.

I believe Candler's story is informed by this understanding of faith. Paraphrasing Candler's core values, Candler *dreams a future* in which its students, with the highest standard of intellectual and theological integrity, are critically and faithfully engaging the Christian tradition, celebrating diversity, promoting an ecumenical vision of the church, and dedicated to social justice.

This prophetic dream is not just fanciful wishing. This dream is a vision of faith that has motivated Candler:

- to have one of the most outstanding faculties in theological education;

- to have one of the largest theological library collections in the world;

- to place students locally and internationally in contexts where the realities of people are known, the challenges of ministry are instructive, and opportunities for service are abundant;

- to establish community life programs and worship services that deepen experiences of community and of God;

---

[3] Candler School of Theology, "Our Mission, Vision & Values," available online at http://candler.emory.edu/about/mission.html.

31

- to create a learning environment that is beautiful and able to utilize the latest technological resources for student learning.

This dream is not pursued with a manual in hand. Neither has the dream been pursued with a record of successive achievements. In my thirty-five years on Candler's faculty, at times we have been clear about what the Lord requires of us; and we have been bewildered by a world that changes faster than our analytical abilities and our curriculum. Still, through faith, we dream . . . and work . . . and pray. What most characterizes how we pursue the dream is not our having a set of answers, but having minds and hearts that ask, seek, and knock for insight and strength. We revise the answers we receive, because we do not stop the process of asking, seeking, and knocking. Through faith, we pursue and revise and pursue.

In his introduction to Pablo Neruda's *Book of Questions*, William O'Daly writes that "our greatest act of faith" may be "living in a state of visionary surrender to the elemental questions, free of the quiet desperation of clinging too tightly to answers."[4] I have known this to be Candler's pedagogy.

As I've said, we do not have a manual to enact this dream. And if we had one, I suspect we would rightly distrust the manual and whoever gave it to us. We do have, however, the means of faith to perceive God active in the world:

- We are surrounded by the cloud of witnesses. No generation has ever had more witnesses as examples and as guides.

- We have exceptional resources for study and instruction.

- We have students who are eager to give their lives to God's desires for them, the church, and the world.

- We have supportive individuals, congregations, and denominational structures.

- We have the privilege to look to Jesus, the pioneer and perfecter of our faith.

With all of this, we are empowered to enact our prophetic dream.

The centennial theme of "Story and Prophecy" provides an apt interpretation of Candler's witness and mission. Declaring prophecy to

---

[4] Pablo Neruda, *The Book of Questions*, translated with introduction by William O'Daly (Port Townsend, WA: Copper Canyon Press, 2001), x.

be foundational to Candler's identity is a bold affirmation, for we then understand ourselves to be reading the times in which we live and to be bearing witness to God's purposes for these times and the times to come. Prophetic action ought to occur even when community realities seem tranquil. Tranquil times provide an atmosphere to pursue God's dream without the pressure and frenzy of crisis. Prophetic action transitions into urgent modes of announcement, organizing, and protest when crises loom.

The crises for our prophetic attention are not just gathering in some distant land and arriving in some unforeseen year. *Now* is the time for our prophetic witness. We have sinful and deadly realities that a faithful people must experience as breaking God's heart—and whatever breaks God's heart must break our hearts:

- Candler resides in a state where 300 to 700 children are commercially sexually exploited every month. And Atlanta is a major hub for this enslavement and torture of our children.

- Candler resides in the most incarcerating nation in the world, where the justice system is imbalanced against the poor, and whole communities are incapacitated because their youth and adults are imprisoned. This is not only a crisis for these communities; this is a crisis for the whole nation.

- Candler resides in a world where 50 percent of its population lives on less than $2.50 a day. And a world where the basic availability of healthy water, air, and agricultural land decreases at alarming rates.

- Candler students and alums reside in churches where members do not know how to have fierce disagreements and still relate to one another in loving ways. And so churches often avoid bearing witness to any issue that is likely to cause conflict—even issues that break God's heart.

These are a few of the realities that must be engaged if Candler's prophetic dreaming is to have credibility in a world that yearns to witness prophetic action. Let us pray that we realize that in the tradition of the biblical prophets, prophetic dreaming occurs with the awareness of urgency. Our core values urge us to run *now* with perseverance the race that is set before us.

The race is not run on a smooth track, but on rough and treacherous ground. It's run in urban areas where many fear to tread, in affluent communities where wealth does not prevent domestic abuse and drug addictions, in hospitals and nursing homes where loved ones and strangers long for visitors, in small towns gasping for economic vitality. The race is run wherever faith, hope, and love are needed.

The race is not only challenging, it can be punishing and deadly. From our text in Hebrews, listen to the list of outcomes that occurred to witnesses who ran the race by faith: torture, mocking, flogging, chains, imprisonment, stoning, put to the sword, destitute, persecuted, tormented. Even Jesus, the pioneer and perfecter of our faith "endured the cross." These are the possible outcomes when one is "betting one's life" on the unseen realities of God . . . when one, by faith, is "all in."

I've talked with pastors who believe that they can be "all in" for God and can opt out of prophetic ministry. These pastors believe that if they haven't claimed a prophetic identity then they are excused from prophetic responsibilities. They consider prophetic ministry to be like an elective course in a school's curriculum—a course that's not required for graduation. When I read the consequences of faith reported in Hebrews, I can appreciate why they have conjured up their exemption status. The truth be told, more Christian clergy, laity, and institutions than we would like to admit, will claim the option of exemption when prophetic ministry goes beyond appreciating the *idea* of prophetic commitment.

Once it is acceptable to exempt oneself from "the race set before us" because it is too scary or difficult or at odds with one's temperament, all forms of ministry are in jeopardy—hospital visits, welcoming strangers, hospitality to recovery groups, loving neighbors. In the early days of Methodism, when children were seen as being an integral part of the small group meetings, some preachers declared "but I have no gift for [working with children]." John Wesley replied, "gift or no gift, you are to do it, else you are not called to be a Methodist preacher."[5]

We should be proud that Candler has embraced prophetic action as an identity of its history and its future. This is inspiring! And we

---

[5] John Wesley, The "Large" *Minutes* (1770–72), Q. 34.3, in *The Works of John Wesley*, vol. 10, *The Methodist Societies: The Minutes of Conference*, ed. Henry D. Rack (Nashville: Abingdon Press, 2011), 889.

can be certain that circumstances will arise that test our resolve to persevere as a prophetic institution.

This centennial celebration year is Candler's effort to cherish its history, but it's about more than telling the stories that have formed us. The gatherings of this centennial year are not a protracted eulogizing of Candler. These centennial celebrations are a call to dream and to prepare and to run with perseverance the race that is set before us.

Perhaps what we are most trying to do this year is to say "thank you." Thank you to the witnesses and all those who have contributed to Candler's story. And the celebration is the outpouring of our hearts in gratitude to God—not just for God being active in our story, but for the privilege of being called to discipleship in God's story.

By faith, we thank you, O God . . . we thank you. We pray that you are delighted by how we bear witness to *your* story and *your* saving message as we run the race that *you* have set before us. Amen.

CHAPTER 5

Reforming Theological Education:
The Story of Women at Candler

Carol A. Newsom

Reformation Day Celebration Lecture
October 21, 2014

The story of women at Candler begins in the era of the TV show
Mad Men: the 1960s. Part of the reason that program was so popular is that it took us back to an era that now seems so alien, even for those of us who can actually remember it. It's the era just at the dawn of the radical change in women's roles in society, a time when blatant discrimination and sexism were simply taken for granted. Gail Collins' wonderful book on this era is aptly entitled *When Everything Changed*.[1]

Before turning to Candler in the 1960s, however, it is important to take a quick look back at an even earlier time. Candler actually voted to admit women as students in 1922, though it was not until 1938 that the first woman grduated with a Bachelor of Divinity degree, Mary Vaughn Johnson, the wife of an assistant professor of church administration. By 1956 only twenty women had been awarded the BD degree, half of them married to Candler students and preparing for the role of minister's wife, since until that year the Methodist church did not ordain women. And it would be another twenty years before the Lutherans and Anglicans approved the ordination of women. So, there was not much demand among women for the degree, though some did use it as a stepping stone toward a PhD and a career teaching religion in colleges. A small but significant number of women did take a Masters of Christian Education

---

[1] Gail Collins, *When Everything Changed: The Amazing Journey of American Women from 1960 to the Present* (New York: Little, Brown, 2009).

degree, however, since that was considered a suitable role for women in the church.

Now, fast forward to 1969, when James T. Laney became the dean of the Candler School of Theology, and a new era began. But not without its growing pains. In 1969 Diane Moseley entered Candler, the only woman in her MDiv class of 140. (In an interview when she received a distinguished alumni award in 2013, she commented that she thought at first the ratio might be God's reward to her for having gone to an all women's college; but it wasn't that simple.) The next year Toni White entered the program, again the only woman. By 1973, when Susan Henry-Crowe entered, we had a population explosion: there were eleven women in the MDiv program — a whopping 3 percent of Candler students! But these were very impressive women.

Candler, however, was not remotely prepared for them. There were no women on the faculty, so they had no one there to give voice to their concerns. Indeed, they had few role models at all. Susan Bishop, who entered at this time, said that she had never even seen an ordained woman when she entered Candler and wasn't entirely convinced they existed. But this group of talented women banded together to support one another and to teach both their male peers and their male faculty members how to make a place for women in this institution and in their theological thinking. Toni White wrote a short paper in 1974 entitled "A Feminine Word to the Men of God," describing the discrimination faced by women in the church and also the exclusion that was created by using language in a way that assumed all people were "men" and certainly all ministers were "men." Indeed, Toni recalls that the sermon that was preached at her ordination was entitled, "Now I Have Become a Man." She nearly refused ordination because she was so distressed at her invisibility to the church. The women students began to talk with their professors about these issues, literally educating them in basic principles of feminist thought. The professors were well intentioned but not always conscious of how their language excluded the very being of women. So, Diane and Toni undertook a bit of street theater to get their message across. I'll let Toni tell the story in her own words.

Do y'all know the apple story? There happened to be ten of us [women] in the systematic theology class, and poor Dr. Runyon

[Theodore Runyon Jr.] had been away on sabbatical for a year— the year in which we had sensitized everybody else to the inclusive language issue. And he came back talking about the "doctrine of man" and not using any inclusive language. We tried to talk to him about it, but he didn't get it. And so on one particular day, all ten of us brought apples into class, and at the beginning of class, one of the women said, "Dr. Runyon—" and presented him with an apple—"Eve wants you to have this." And every time he used a sexist word, we would all—*crunch!*—take a bite out of our apple. Well, it immediately polarized the class and the student body. The men who supported us thought it was a hilarious and great idea for sensitizing him. The other men in the class thought that it was very abusive, and that we were "strident feminists" and that it should never have happened. So it sort of polarized the school. But that was one of the ways that we got our point across.[2]

The women of the 1970s also tell the "restroom occupation" story. The architects of Bishops Hall did not envision it being home to many women—just the secretaries. The only women's restroom was located in a fairly remote part of the building, at some distance from the main classrooms. The women students complained about running up and down three flights of stairs between classes. When their initial appeal to have the women's restroom relocated to the main floor went unheeded, they staged a sit-in, put a big "Women's" sign on the door of one of the men's restrooms, and worked out a schedule of thirty-minute shifts, insuring that a woman was present in that restroom at all hours of the day. The women's restroom was soon relocated to a more convenient spot. Many years later, when the need for a second women's restroom became evident from the long lines at the first, one of the men's restrooms was reassigned for women—only nobody thought to take out the urinals! So the women were reminded daily that this was a building that had just never anticipated their presence.

---

[2] Susan Bishop, Michelle Holmes Chaney, Elizabeth Tapia, and Toni White, "Challenging Stories, Remembering the Past, Dreaming the Future," transcript of Oral History Panel Discussion, Candler School of Theology, 25 October 2006. The Women in Theology and Ministry Oral History Project, CSTA 015, Archives and Manuscript Department, Pitts Theology Library, Emory University, p. 4 (of 37).

By 1974 the women had formed a Women's Caucus and they presented their concerns to the faculty.[3] They included these six points:

(1) Set a goal to raise the percentage of women students from 5 percent to 50 percent. (Candler reached that goal in 2000 and it has been a steady figure ever since.)

(2) Restructure the experience of Supervised Ministry (the predecessor of Contextual Education) to include more women supervisors, additional placement sites for exposure to women's crisis situations, and the placement of not fewer than two women or two minority persons per Supervised Ministry group. As Susan Bishop, a member of the Women's Caucus, said at the time, "Practical skills of ministry to and with women have to be acquired in spite of rather than because of the curriculum at Candler." By the end of the decade, when Phyllis Roe, a 1978 graduate, became the director of Supervised Ministry, Candler was beginning to address these issues.

(3) Appoint a woman to the faculty and continue hiring women in faculty and administrative positions until the ratio of women to men approximates the ratio of women to men in the church. Candler still hasn't reached that goal, though women faculty and administrators are now a powerful presence.

(4) Integrate women's studies into all courses as well as provide offerings in the area of women's studies.

(5) Create a faculty-student committee to evaluate the seminary experience of women and other minorities, make recommendations for policy changes and program implementation for women and minorities, and act as a mediator in discriminatory situations involving women and minorities. (It was not until 1988–89 that such a committee was established.)

(6) Deal with the problem of language, especially the equating of minister and male. (It was only in 1987 that Candler adopted its inclusive language covenant.)

By the end of the decade of the 1970s the number of women had swelled to nearly 20 percent of the student body, which, as social psychologists tell us, is a critical number for being a true presence at

[3] "A Brief Her/History of the Program for Women in Theology and Ministry," compiled by Helen Burch Pearson, November 8, 1998. Program for Women in Theology and Ministry records, CSTA 014, Box 3, Folder 10, Archives and Manuscripts Department, Pitts Theology Library, Emory University.

an institution. But the issues were much the same as they had been in 1974. In 1978, the Women's Caucus issued an open letter to the faculty expressing their concerns. One paragraph, in particular, highlights the immense burdens on this courageous group of women.

> When it comes to role models, we women are at a loss. Either we live constantly with the pressure of creating something new, or we try in some manner to put on men's shoes that simply don't fit. To have the opportunity to learn and know about other women in our field of endeavor could give us some understanding of the background of our presence in the church, as well as encourage our male colleagues to reflect on their attitudes and behavior toward women.[4]

This is not to say, of course, that the women had been without any support. Dean Laney brought in Peggy Billings from New York to teach a course on feminist theology. Betsy Lunz also taught two courses on women and religion. Nor was all of the work on including women done by women. Walt Lowe taught the first course ever offered by a full-time Candler faculty member on feminist theology. Nancy Hardesty, church historian and coauthor of the influential evangelical feminist work, *All We're Meant to Be: Biblical Feminism for Today,*[5] also taught at Candler in the late 1970s, though not in a tenure track position, and she soon left to pursue a speaking and writing career. So, for the most part, the Candler women of the 1970s were forging their own path. They were truly re-forming Candler.

The best way I can suggest how extraordinary these women were and are is to choose just a few of them and tell you about the exceptional and creative ministries they have forged for themselves.

Diane Moseley (MDiv 1973), who was honored in 2013 as one of Candler's distinguished alumni, found her passion in ministry at Killingsworth Home, a residential facility for women in crisis—women leaving abusive relationships, women struggling with alcohol or drug dependency, women who are victims of rape and sexual

---

[4] "Open Letter to the Faculty," May 2, 1978. Program for Women in Theology and Ministry records, CSTA 014, Box 3, Folder 10, Archives and Manuscripts Department, Pitts Theology Library, Emory University. The letter was signed by forty-four women.

[5] Letha Dawson Scanzoni and Nancy A. Hardesty, *All We're Meant to Be: Biblical Feminism for Today* (Waco, TX: Word Books, 1974).

abuse, women living with mental illness. When receiving her distinguished alumni award she described her passion for this ministry as "a holy energy and a fierce desire to be part of the journey to love and justice."

Susan Bishop (MDiv 1975) is one of the most extraordinary individuals ever graduated from the Candler School of Theology, male or female. A Southern Baptist, she came to Emory in 1972 never having seen an ordained woman. She almost dropped out after her first quarter. Her urgency for ministry didn't quite connect with the courses she was taking. But during the winter she attended a Women Seminarian's conference in Virginia that brought together some of the women across the country who were truly the first significant generation of women in theological education, and she was transfixed. There she encountered for the first time women who actually were ordained! She met the women who were creating feminist theology, including Rosemary Radford Reuther and Mary Daly. Some of them, like Mary Daly, were a bit frightening in their radicalness, but they were exciting. This was her "aha moment." But it was not just women who sustained Susan. She credits both Dean Jim Laney and Associate Dean Jim Waits (later Dean of Candler) as critical mentors for her. We should never underestimate the vision of these two deans who saw the importance of women before many on the faculty recognized this issue.

Like many of the other women at Candler in the early 1970s, Susan had a better idea of why she wanted to study theology than she did of what she was supposed to do with that education. She was clearly drawn to working with marginalized people (that is a hallmark of many of these women, and perhaps not unrelated to their own experience), and was offered a job at New Horizons, a work release center for women. It clicked. Eventually, Susan would serve as chaplain to three different prisons, mostly those for incarcerated women. Susan was a trained musician and choral director, and so she began to develop women's choirs in the prisons, not just giving the women an organized activity, but also providing a way that they could interact with the "outside" world. Susan's choir from Metro State Prison for Women and now the Arrendale Prison is called "Voices of Hope," a perfect name for the essence of her ministry with these women. They are an extraordinary choir and have had some exceptionally talented members. Susan's work attracted the attention of

Emily Saliers, one of the Indigo Girls (and a daughter of Candler's own Don Saliers), and Emily has helped talented members of the choir to develop professional careers in music.

Susan and Candler's ethics professor Liz Bounds created an educational program within the prison—a certificate program in theological studies. Candler faculty, Graduate Division of Religion students, and Candler students have all taught in this program, which everyone describes as transformative, both for the inmates and for those who teach these exceptional women. A few years ago, as I was reading over the admissions essays of my new advisees, I was struck by the admissions statement of one of them. She had been in the Metro State Prison for Women and had done the theology certificate and was now a student at Candler. Without Susan's ministry, none of this would have happened. Without Candler's decision in the early 1970s to train these women like Susan, none of this could have happened.

Some of the women Candler trained during these years have focused their ministries on Emory itself and have continued to form and reform our community. I want to mention two of them. First, Susan Henry-Crowe. Susan entered Candler in 1973, so she was of that first generation of women at Candler. Somewhat surprisingly, the South Carolina Conference seems to have been one of the most progressive in supporting women in ministry in the 1970s. When Susan graduated in in 1976, she was given a two point charge in rural South Carolina, not an easy place for a woman minister. One of the congregations was opposed to her coming; the other was just desperate to have an appointed minister at all. Susan discerned one thing quickly. Every minister earns her or his "cred" by being present in pastoral situations. And she was there—when people were sick, when funerals needed to be conducted (even during what should have been her vacation), whenever there was need. And before long, she was beloved. But her administrative talents were also quickly recognized by the conference, and so she was drawn into administrative roles. Then, in 1991, she was named as the first woman to be Chaplain and Dean of the Chapel and Religious Life at Emory University. She was an ideal appointment for this school at this time.

Two qualities that Susan exemplified served this university well. First, Susan was able to be a calm presence in conflict and knew how to bring parties together. She and Sammy Clark, the chaplain for

Emory's Oxford Campus, found a Solomonic resolution to the crisis that erupted over whether same-sex couples could have commitment ceremonies in Emory chapels, since United Methodist rules did not permit such ceremonies. Susan and Sammy made the important distinction that university chapels were not denominational churches and that universities accredited many different religious bodies to use their facilities. So, they reasoned, each accredited denomination should be able to use the chapel for the religious ceremonies sanctioned by its own denomination. It was a solution that all parties readily agreed to.

Susan also discovered, even when she was in high school and attended a United Nations seminar that happened to coincide with the Six-Day War in 1967, that she was passionately interested in the world and all its difference, but especially its religious differences. So, when Susan came to Emory, Emory was also experiencing changes in enrollment patterns that would make it one of the most religously diverse campuses in the United States. There are significant numbers of Hindus, Muslims, Buddhists, Jews, and Christians — and within the Christian community, of Catholics, mainline Protestants, Evangelicals, Pentecostals, and Nondenominationals — and now the Seekers and the Nones. Susan's love of being in the betwixt and between had made her the ideal Dean of Religious Life to help the various student groups both to establish robust forms of cohort-building worship in their own traditions and also to make sure they engaged in inter-religious dialogue. Susan has also used her unique role to foster women in other religous traditions who are tracing a trajectory similar to that of women within Christianity in the nineteenth and twentieth centuries. She mentors young Islamic women who cannot be ordained as imams, urging them to pursue PhDs in religion and make an impact, so that the next generation of women can be ordained, just as Christian women came to Candler with those goals in the 1950s.

Susan's impact within The United Methodist Church has also been extraordinary, as she became a member of the church's Judicial Council in 1992 and the president of that body in 2008. Susan left Emory in 2014 to become the General Secretary of the General Board of Church and Society, The United Methodist Church's main arm for social justice and advocacy, education, and international outreach. Not bad for a woman who was the second-ever woman ever to serve as a full-time pastor in South Carolina. A lot can change within a generation.

The other Candler woman from the same era whose career has graced Emory is Nan Baxter. She graduated somewhat later, in 1980, one of our early Anglican/Episcopal women students at Emory, a group that has also made an outsized impact in ministry. The Episcopal church had only been ordaining women since the mid 1970s, so there was still a lot of resistance. Claiborne Jones, also a Candler graduate, who was ordained in 1979, says that when she and another woman were the second and third women to be ordained in the Atlanta diocese, they were referred to by some male priests as "priestitutes," a small marker of the sexism that these women had to endure. Their bishop supported the ordination of women but did not always perceive the cost. He assigned Nan for her first year of student internship to a high-profile church that had explicitly said it did not want a woman. She survived, and in fact had a powerful impact there, much to the consternation of the reactionary clergy.

Nan once told me she thought she was given her next assignment—to inaugurate the Episcopal Chaplaincy program at Emory—as partial compensation for that hellish first-year assignment. Whatever her bishop's motives may have been, he gave Emory a singular gift. Nan not only shepherded Emory's Episcopalian undergraduates, but along with Ted Hackett she also provided supervision for Candler's Episcopalian students. Approximately one-third of the currently serving Episcopal clergy in the Atlanta diocese are Candler graduates, and Nan Baxter supervised and guided most of them in their training for ministry.

Part of Nan's work was also ministry in the Wesley Woods Geriatric Center, an affiliate of Emory University. She nurtured worshiping communities there for over twenty-five years, and as she herself reached retirement age, she began to envision a new ministry that would focus on what she called "godly aging." Together with some other female Episcopal clergy and lay members, she founded the religious Society of St. Anna the Prophet, "dedicated to Godly aging and elder ministry."[6] Their work at Wesley Woods has been to help the participating residents there "begin to understand the necessity

---

[6] For information about the Society of St. Anna the Prophet see the Society's website at http://annasisters.org/.

of living in care as a new possibility for living in Christian community" and "to define their experience of old age not as curse but as blessing."

In my recounting of the heroines of the women of the 1970s you may or may not have noticed one thing—they were all white. Candler did have African American students in the 1970s but they were mostly male. Women and persons of color were making their entry into Candler at about the same time. But the presence of women of color was a slightly later phenomenon. A few African American women attended Candler in the 1980s, but it was in the 1990s and beyond that their numbers have increased and they have become such an important presence here. Their struggles overlapped with those of the white women but were also different in significant ways. In 1994 they found their voice in an important statement to the community that involved some consciousness raising for their white sisters, as well as for the Candler community at large. This group of women was led by Kimberly Detherage and supported by Belle Miller McMaster, the faculty director of Candler's Women in Theology and Ministry program at the time. While some African American women were active in Candler's Women's caucus, it did not address all of their needs, and so, Candler's first female African American professor, Teresa Fry Brown, helped these women establish Sistah Circle, a group that focused the concerns and interests of the African American women.

These women, too, have been making a profound impact in the church and the world. Many are bringing women's pastoral leadership not only to local churches but also to the denominations as a whole. Telley Gadson was recently elected as the national president of Black Clergy Women of The United Methodist Church, and Kimberly Detherage is now president of the AME Church's Women in Ministry. Detherage practiced law for twenty years and owned her own law firm in New York before coming to Candler. She pastors St. Mark's AME Church in Jackson Heights, New York, and has held a number of leadership posts within the AME Church, as well as coauthoring legislation on clergy and lay sexual misconduct and providing numerous workshops on the implementation of those policies.

African American women graduates of Candler have also made an impact on higher education. No fewer than five hold academic posts: Maria Dixon Hall at SMU, Tamaura Lomax at Virginia Commonwealth University, Stacey Floyd Thomas at Vanderbilt Divinity School, Maisha Handy at the Interdenominational Theological Center, and Roslyn Satchel at Pepperdine. Let me tell you about Roslyn Satchel, who is not only an academic but a leader in the field of human rights and child advocacy. Named by *Ebony* magazine in 2005 as one of the "30 Young Leaders of the Future," she did the joint MDiv/JD program at Emory, completing it in a record four and one-half years. Following graduation she was a Soros Justice Fellow at the Southern Center for Human Rights and worked on litigation against the State of Georgia Department of Corrections to improve conditions for incarcerated youth. She is the founding director of DESIST, an advocacy organization for children in juvenile court systems. And she served as the executive director of the National Center for Human Rights Education. Now, having completed her PhD in communications from LSU, she has joined the faculty of Pepperdine University.

I've been telling the story of women at Candler primarily through its students, but the story of the women faculty at Candler is also important. I am the second tenured woman ever to have been hired at Candler. The first, Roberta Bondi, was hired just one year before me. In many ways it is incredible to think that Candler is still in its "first generation" of women faculty. But it is true. Roberta had a good job at Notre Dame teaching Semitic languages. She came to her interview at Candler with a great reluctance, mistrustful of the church, which had in many ways been a wounding institution for her. But she wanted to teach patristics more than Semitic languages, and so she accepted the position. Perhaps as an unconscious signal of Candler's lack of readiness for its first female tenure-track faculty member, the faculty meeting minutes announcing her appointment misspelled her name. Roberta was on the search committee the next year when a search for an Old Testament professor was announced. I had not intended to apply for jobs that year. I had just started work on my dissertation—a critical edition of one of the Dead Sea Scrolls—and had been awarded a fellowship that would have paid for a year in Israel. But this job came open unexpectedly, in April, and one of my faculty advisors strongly urged me to apply. The Candler faculty was, at that time, somewhat ambivalent about women academics. They weren't hostile, but it was difficult for some of them to perceive us as serious scholars. After all, they'd never seen any before! Both Roberta and I found out, shortly after we came, that the vote in our academic areas (historical theology in her case, biblical studies in mine) had gone against us, 4 to 1 in my case. But Deans Laney and Waits and a progressive group in the faculty knew that it was time—and way past time—for women to be appointed to the faculty. And so we were offered jobs. And I will be ever grateful for their support and encouragement. But it was four more years before the next woman was hired: Nancy Ammerman in sociology of religion (1984). Finally, in 1986–87, four more women were hired: Jane McAuliffe in world religions, Rebecca Chopp in theology, Susan Garrett in New Testament, and Gail O'Day in homiletics. At last, a peer group!

When I asked some of these women about their recollections of "the early days" and how they experienced both support and resistance, I found that memories were different. Everyone agreed that Cander was fundamentally a good and supportive environment, but two of the women remembered more incidents that reflected the reluctance of some faculty colleagues to acknowledge women's place in theological education or that reflected their simple awkward cluelessness. Everyone remembered the day when four or five of us were having lunch in the faculty dining room and a male colleague came up and said, "So what are you ladies conspiring about?" It did not go over well with us and reminded us that we still made some of the male faculty nervous by our very presence.

I think that the different ways we recollect our experience of the early years had as much to do with what we brought as it did with the context within which we worked. Those of us who were fortunate enough to have fathers and other early male mentors who encouraged us and believed we could and should do anything we aspired to tended to perceive the support at Candler and brush off the occasional patronizing attitudes or slights. Those who had not received that critical early support were more sensitive to the negative encounters, as they reinforced the sense of having to struggle against male doubt about their abilities and their right to a place at the table.

In general, however, it was not the faculty who had major adjustments to make, but the male students. When Roberta and I came, the student body was still about 82 percent male, and on the whole, much more conservative than the faculty. For some of them, the idea of women as authorities in religious matters was, well, an abomination! One male student refused to attend class on the days when Roberta lectured in the Introduction to Church History course that she co-taught with William (Bill) Mallard. I repeatedly experienced having my authority challenged by male students in the classroom and at one point was told by women students that a male student was saying terrible things about me and, in their opinion, making only thinly veiled threats against me. These days such behavior would quickly become the subject of an investigation. But we pioneer women were tough, and I just thanked them for the information — and kept my eyes open. One of the ways we supported one another was the establishment of a weekly breakfast group that included the two women faculty, a few Candler grads who had been hired by Candler to administrative posts, and two graduate students. We called ourselves the "Hot Cross Buns." You have to have humor.

Just as the first generation of women students at Candler have had remarkable careers, so the first generation of Candler women faculty have done some extraordinary things. One of the most striking things is that Candler has been its role as an incubator for preparing women for leadership in academic administration. Deans Waits, LaGree, and Richey all appointed women to serve as the associate dean for academic affairs. And each of these women used that administrative experience as a stepping stone to exceptional careers in academic leadership. Jane McAuliffe became the dean of Georgetown University and then the president of Bryn Mawr College. Rebecca Chopp became provost of Emory University, dean of Yale Divinity School, president of Colgate University, president of Swarthmore College, and now chancellor of the University of Denver. Candler women have also gone on to be leaders in theological education, too, with Gail O'Day now serving as the dean of Wake Forest's School of Theology. Although Mary Elizabeth Moore did not serve a term as Candler's academic dean (more on her role shortly), she also went on to become the dean of Boston University School of Theology. This is a simply astonishing record of achievement at the highest levels.

Candler women also wrote and edited important books that advanced scholarship in many directions — and here I will focus just on a couple of those having to do with feminist theology and hermeneutics. Rebecca Chopp's research during the 1980s led to a critical book in feminist theology, *The Power to Speak: Feminism, Language, and God.*[7] A decade later she turned her attention to feminist theological education itself in her book, *Saving Work: Feminist Practices of Theological Education.*[8] What she and others of our generation were trying to bring into being she put into words. While one could tell the story of women at Candler as women's transformation of Candler, it is important to recognize Candler's transformation of women. Rebecca says in her introduction to the book that in graduate school and in her early formation in the guild, she had been warned away from too close an identification with feminist theology. It could be bad for your career. But once she was here, actually trying to educate women and men from a commitment to the full inclusion of women's experience, writing about feminist issues became imperative.

I experienced the same phenomenon. My training and research was in the Dead Sea Scrolls, not feminist theology. But in 1989 a savvy editor from Westminster John Knox Press, Cynthia Thompson, approached me about possibly editing a one-volume commentary on the Bible featuring feminist biblical hermeneutics. When I immediately declined, she changed tactics. She asked if I would just write a memorandum in which I outlined what I might like to see in such a volume, what I might find useful for my teaching. She knew what she was doing. As I wrote the memo, I realized that I wanted to be part of this project. As a result, the press asked Sharon Ringe, a New Testament scholar from Wesley Theological Seminary, and me to put together what we decided to call the *Women's Bible Commentary.*[9] At the time—the mid-to-late 1980s—we weren't sure we could find enough women to cover all of the biblical books: feminist biblical hermeneutics was in its early stages. And, in fact, it was a bit of a scrape for the first edition. It was certainly my education in feminist biblical hermeneutics.

Our first edition in 1992 produced a combination of accolades

---

[7] Rebecca S. Chopp, *The Power to Speak: Feminism, Language, and God* (New York: Crossroad, 1989).

[8] Rebecca S. Chopp, *Saving Work: Feminist Practices of Theological Education* (Louisville: Westminster John Knox, 1995).

[9] Carol A. Newsom and Sharon H. Ringe, eds., *Women's Bible Commentary* (Louisville: Westminster John Knox, 1992). The title was an allusion to Elizabeth Cady Stanton's famous *Woman's Bible* (1895–1898).

and excoriation, which was pretty much what we anticipated. An expanded edition was published in 1998, because we realized that the book was also having an important impact in Catholic circles, and we wanted to include the fascinating materials about women in the books Protestants call the Apocrypha and Catholics include in their canon.[10] Sharon and I thought that the *Women's Bible Commentary* would have a shelf life of five to ten years or so and then be replaced by other works. Other works appeared, but they didn't seem to displace the *WBC*, which kept on selling. We passed the 100,000 sales mark some time ago. So, we decided it was time for a twentieth anniversary edition. Adding a third editor, Jacq Lapsley, an Emory graduate, we produced a thoroughly revised and updated edition, bringing in a more diverse and theoretically up to date roster of authors, while keeping some of the classic essays from our first edition.[11] This time we didn't have to scrape to find authors. We were distraught that there were so many we could not include.

Just as with my story about the female students at Candler, you will note that I have been talking about white female faculty. What about women of color? Similarly, that was a story that developed at a somewhat later time. Candler had actually had several black male professors, beginning in the 1970s with Grant Shockley and then Noel Erskine and Luther Smith, and in the 1980s Romney Moseley and Robert Franklin. But we had no black women. It was not until 1994 that Candler hired Teresa Fry Brown as a professor of homiletics. Just as the first generation of white women were overachievers, so Professor Fry Brown has been. She has been one of the most important academic—and practical—interpreters of black women's voices in the African American church. The titles of her books tell their own story: *God Don't Like Ugly: African American Women Handing on Spiritual Values* (2000); *Weary Throats and New Songs: Black Women Proclaiming God's Word* (2003); and *Can A Sistah Get a Little*

---

[10] Carol A. Newsom and Sharon H. Ringe, eds., *Women's Bible Commentary*, expanded ed. with Apocrypha (Louisville: Westminster John Knox, 1998).

[11] Carol A. Newsom, Sharon H. Ringe, and Jacqueline E. Lapsley, eds., *Women's Bible Commentary*, rev. ed. (Louisville: Westinster John Knox, 2012).

Help? Advice and Encouragement for Black Women in Ministry (2008).[12] Teresa has, like her sisters in Candler's MDiv program, also been a leader in the AME Church, being elected in 2012 to the prestigious post of historiographer and editor of the *AME Review*. Teresa's impact is also figured by her schedule, because she is so much in demand. Catching Teresa to schedule a meeting is somewhat like catching the snitch in a game of Quidditch at Hogwarts—she is that golden object always flying between one place and another.

Although her impact on Candler was great, Teresa worked without another African American female colleague until 2008, when Candler hired Andrea White in systematic theology. Since then, Nichole Phillips has been hired in sociology of religion (2013) and Khalia Williams in worship (2015). A peer group at last? Some forty years after women began to come to Candler? The number has a certain biblical resonance.

Telling the story by means of students and faculty is vitally important, but there are also institutional stories to be told. One of these is the history of the administrative staff. Long before students graduated from Candler with an MDiv, women were serving in—often underpaid and undervalued—positions on Candler's staff, but they were nevertheless instrumental in shaping the ethos of Candler. Even before Candler had many female MDiv graduates there were the "three Helens"—Helen Banks, coordinator of supervised ministry; Helen Myler, the registrar; and Helen Stowers, the director of student aid and services. No one who knew them can ever forget Betty Smith, the formidable but infinitely funny administrative assistant to Dean Waits, or Marilyn McManaway, the savvy and amazingly organized administrative assistant to the academic dean. And there are many others I could name.

Early on, as Candler began to graduate women students, their annual conferences were not keen to place them in local church appointments. Candler hired several of these women onto its own administrative staff—Nelia Kimbrough, who served as assistant to the dean (and who went on to have an extraordinary ministry in

---

[12] Teresa L. Fry Brown, *God Don't Like Ugly: African American Women Handing on Spiritual Values* (Nashville: Abingdon Press, 2000); *Weary Throats and New Songs: Black Women Proclaiming God's Word* (Nashville: Abingdon Press, 2003); *Can A Sistah Get a Little Help? Advice and Encouragement for Black Women in Ministry* (New York: Pilgrim Press, 2008).

forming intentional Christian communities in service to the poor and homeless); Phyllis Roe, director of Supervised Ministries (one of my "Hot Cross Buns" buddies, who went on to found the first inter-religious pastoral care center in Hawaii); Susan Laird Puckett, dean of students in the 1980s; and Helen Pearson, dean of Community Life. These and many others who have followed them have enriched our life together.

Candler, though not without its own problems, became a kind of oasis. Here women students could experience a welcoming context in which their gifts were recognized and encouraged. However, once they went out into the local church contexts, many women experienced degrees of sexism and rejection of their work that they had not anticipated. Clearly Candler was not fully educating its women students if we were not preparing and supporting them for this transition. This is the story of the program in Women, Theology, and Ministry. This program actually had its roots back in the work of the Women's Caucus of the 1970s and 1980s. Initially, its focus was Candler oriented, as we still needed resources to teach women students. Beginning in 1985 the Women's Caucus began sponsoring Women's Week programing, bringing in high profile feminist theologians and church leaders for some very powerful events, as well as developing other resources. But the Women's Caucus was a student organization, and Candler needed to make an institutional commitment.

What became the Women, Theology, and Ministry program was first formed in 1990 as the Women's Studies program. Since there was no woman faculty member available to head it up, it was initially directed by a PhD student, Kris Kvam, now a faculty member at St. Paul's School of Theology. When Candler hired Pam Couture in 1991 as professor of pastoral care, part of her portfolio— funded by a temporary grant—was the newly renamed Women in Theology and Ministry program. Pam was succeeded during 1993–1995 by Belle Miller McMaster, a seasoned religious administrator from the Presbyterian Church, who subsequently supervised Candler's Advanced Studies Program. The Women in Theology and Ministry program, for all its excellence, was, however, a study in institutional instability with too much transition in leadership, despite the excellence of the persons who had lead it. It began to achieve stability in 1995 with Helen Pearson, whose long experience at Candler, first as a student and later as the dean of Community Life, gave her insight into institutional dynamics. Helen became a strong advocate for Candler's full ownership of the program, which would be manifested in the intentional hiring of a faculty member to give it leadership. Candler listened, and in 1999 Mary Elizabeth Moore was hired and given the institutional infrastructure that the program needed to flourish.

While the program had been founded to provide resources for women at Candler, by the time Mary Elizabeth took over as director, it had became clear that the critical issue was not the experience at Candler itself, but the experience of women after they left the protective environs of Candler. How could they be prepared while here, and then supported in the more challenging roles they would face in the isolation of parish appointments, often in small towns with few welcoming colleagues or other peer support networks? These concerns continue to be a part of what is now known as the Women, Theology, and Ministry program, but the directors since 2009, Karen Scheib and Ellen Shepherd, have shifted some of the emphases of the program to a new agenda that connects the traditional concerns of the program with emerging interests among women in the church — advocacy for women and children in contexts of economic and sexual oppression. Their leadership is providing the new arc in what has become a vital part of Candler's engagement with women — barely a generation old, but already making a significant impact in the lives of Candler women and men.

The final institutional milestone to be noted, of course is the appointment of Jan Love as the dean of the Candler School of Theology in 2007. She was a nontraditional appointment, someone not ordained, and trained as a political scientist rather than as a theologian, but a committed lay person of the church and an administrator with a remarkable track record. During the interview process, both President Jim Wagner and Provost Earl Lewis became passionately persuaded that they had to have Jan for Candler and for Emory. Since I have been at Candler for nearly thirty-four years, I have become something of a connoisseur of deans. Each of the deans I have served under has been excellent, each one advancing Candler's mission in vital ways. And in the rapidly changing context of the church and theological education in the twenty- first century, Jan Love is the ideal dean for Candler.

I have told only the smallest part of the story of women and the reformation of theological education at Candler over the past fifty years. That story continues to develop. As Candler becomes more diverse, new generations of women raise new issues about their place in theological education and in the church, as they seek full recognition of their ministries. Hispanic, Korean, Chinese, and African women at Candler remind us that their presence will bring new transformations and further enrichment of the school and the church. Their stories are just beginning to unfold. And, unfortunately, there are some stories that often cannot be told, those of LGBTQ women, who still struggle for full inclusion in many denominations. The process of transformation is a continuing one, however, and if we were to upate this account ten years from now, I hope we would see the full recognition of all women's leadership within the church, within theological education, and throughout the world.

CHAPTER 6

Close to the Heart of Humankind

Steven M. Tipton

Spring Convocation Address
January 13, 2015

Methodism girdles the globe. It does infinitely more than that. It lies close to the heart of humankind."[1] So wrote Jacob Riis a century ago. He wrote from firsthand experience as a crusading journalist and social reformer, inspired by Methodist revivals to save souls and by its Social Gospel to save cities.

That was then, and this is now. What happened in between? A century ago one in three Americans still worked on family farms, and they lived little more than fifty years on average. Today only one in a hundred Americans labor on farms, we live some eighty years on average, and there are four times as many of us here.[2] How have changes in the way we live and the way we pray come together in Methodism over this century? That's a good centennial question to ask in light of a timeless one: What must we do to be saved? For the answer lies in a whole way of life, not in this or that good deed or burnt sacrifice. What does it mean to do justly, love mercy, and walk humbly with thy God in biblical Jerusalem, *and* down these uneven streets in this promised land? (Mic 6:8)? What does it mean to know the providence of our progress, the covenant of our Constitution, the sacred souls of our sovereign selves?

Think for a moment of the Social Creed that the Methodist Epis-

---

[1] Jacob Riis, "Methodism Lies Close to the Heart of Mankind," *North-western Christian Advocate, Wesley Bicentennial Number* (Chicago: June 17, 1903), 11, quoted in "The Religious World: A Symposium on John Wesley," *The Literary Digest*, vol. 27, no. 1 (July 4, 1903), 17. Cf. Charles W. Keysor, *Our Methodist Heritage* (Elgin, IL: D. C. Cook, 1973), 25.

[2] Claude S. Fischer and Michael Hout, *A Century of Difference* (New York: Russell Sage Foundation, 2006), chap. 5.

copal Church led in proclaiming in 1908. The Church stands for "equal rights and complete justice" for all persons in all stations of life. It stands for fair conciliation and arbitration in economic conflict; for abolishing sweatshops, and the exploitation of women and children; for reasonable hours of labor, with work for all, leisure for all, and a seventh day for all to really rest. It stands for a living wage in every industry and the highest possible reward for our hard work through fairly dividing labor and sharing its fruits. The Church stands for following "the Golden Rule" as the moral measure of our laws, and coming to know "the mind of Christ" as the true guide to our daily way of life.[3]

That was then, and this is now. And today, in fact, living out this creed is no less charged by the fierce urgency of now. The American economy has grown by two-thirds since 1980, and two-thirds of this gain from our common labor has gone to the wealthiest one in a hundred of our households. High-school educated, hourly wage workers, black and white, earn one-sixth less today than they did in 1972. One in four young men of color today goes jobless, one in ten goes to jail; and too, too many go to the morgue yet again and again.

There is enough good work that needs to be done for all of us to share in its doing, for our common good and the good of God's creation. There is enough wealth in a land where one in three families own nothing for all of us to share in the fruit of our labors through living wages, like those who labor in the vineyard, like those who hear the prophet promise that they will build houses and dwell in them, and not lose them to another (Matt 20:1-16; Isa 65:21-22). And so the church has urged and promised us, through the Great Depression and the postwar boom, through stagflation and jobless recovery, right up to the present of the Great Recession and its slow passing. The church persists in calling for public and private cooperation to plan and invest in our future, to protect the future of our planet in peril, and to care for all of this planet's people as God's children.

A century ago, "the War to end all wars" broke out. Many American Methodists stood up for neutrality, then answered the call to arms for God and country as a Christian duty "to save the world for

---

[3] *The Doctrines and Discipline of the Methodist Episcopal Church, 1908* (New York: Eaton & Mains, 1908), 480.

democracy." After Belleau Wood, the Argonne, and the Armistice, Methodism also answered the call to lead a crusade for peace. In 1924 the Methodist Episcopal Church set up the Commission on World Peace. In 1939 the newly reunited Methodist Church took "its stand undivided in opposition to the spirit of war now raging in the world," and after Pearl Harbor the bishops condemned "the processes of war even while accepting the awful alternative, not of our own making, forced upon us by the selfishness and perversity of men."[4]

Before the war was over, the Methodist bishops began "a crusade for a new world order" of peace and justice that helped give birth to the United Nations. Through Korea, Vietnam, the arms race, 9/11, Iraq, and the War on Terror the church has pressed onward in the long twilight struggle to seek a just and lasting peace. "We condemn all acts of terrorism, with no exception for the target or the source," declared the General Conference in the year 2000, and "we oppose the use of indiscriminate military force to combat terrorism." True security "lies not in weapons of war," wrote a majority of Methodist bishops after the Iraq invasion, "but in enabling the poor, the vulnerable, the marginalized to flourish as beloved daughters and sons of God."[5]

That was then, and this is now. Has the final word of peace and justice been spoken, and are we all agreed? Not quite, nor will it ever be in the priesthood of all believers and the self-government of all citizens upon this earth. Connectional, itinerant, and episcopal, the manifold ecclesiology of Methodism can clarify conflicts and reshape them, even if it cannot always resolve them fully. We are "a connectional church because we're first a conciliar church," as Bishop Yeakel put it to the Board of Church and Society. We are freely "fettered to Christ" and bound to one another in Christ,

---

[4] *The Doctrines and Discipline of The Methodist Church, 1939* (New York: Methodist Publishing House, 1939), 698; Methodist Bishops, "Wartime Message of the Council of Bishops," *The Christian Advocate* (January 1, 1942), 7–8.

[5] *The Book of Resolutions of The United Methodist Church, 2000* (Nashville: United Methodist Publishing House, 2000), 787; United Methodist Bishops, "A Call to Repentance and Peace with Justice" (November, 2005), document available on the website of the Florida Conference of The United Methodist Church, http://www.flumc.org /acalltorepentanceandpeacewithjustice.

through a gracious and grace-filled relationship entered into prayerfully before God. This enables us to "go on in affection" with a love that heeds everyone and gives everything and inspires nothing less in return, but *demands* nothing at all as quid-pro-quo—not least always getting our own way or getting the last word. A connectional church "counsels together to know what God would have us do." It knows that creeds and confessions "help us in our lives of worship together." But it also knows that "God has not spoken the last word," and that "when we counsel together the counsel of God is with us."[6]

Can we counsel together now to make moral sense of the denominational numbers game? For more than a century, America has been riding a great wave of rising population while lengthening the ride of a lifetime—and Methodism has flourished. Then, in the 1960s, baby boomers start to drop out, turn on, and tune in, or so the story goes. That old-time religion gets born again, and mainline denominations wake up to find millions of alumni—six million of them Methodist—graduated and gone from church, and now swearing that they are profoundly "spiritual" but not particularly religious.[7]

For more than a generation, in fact, the rising, dipping, and now steadying numbers on mainline church rolls have traced the lines of larger demographic changes as Americans live longer, marry later, and raise fewer children in more dual-career families. More than three-fourths of the statistical variance in mainline membership over the past century runs along these demographic lines. Conservative evangelical churches over the last few decades are now following in our footsteps as their members, too, spend more years studying in school, starting careers, living on their own, and seeking a "soul mate for life" before they settle down to start families of their own.[8]

This changing story of how we live and how we pray underlines

---

[6] Steven M. Tipton, *Public Pulpits* (Chicago: University of Chicago Press, 2007), 135–36.

[7] See Steven M. Tipton, *Getting Saved from the Sixties* (Berkeley: University of California Press, 1982); Robert Wuthnow, *After the Baby Boomers* (Princeton: Princeton University Press, 2007); Pew Research Center, "Faith in Flux: Changes in Religious Affiliation in the U.S." (2009), available online at http://www.pewforum.org/datasets/faith-in-flux-changes-in-religious-affiliation-in-the-u-s/.

[8] Barbara Dafoe Whitehead and David Popenoe, "Who Wants to Marry

the church's need to make disciples, not just members. It underscores the denomination's need to "let the church be the church" in the liberated vigor and diversity of its expression in local congregations at worship, witness, and communion across the lines of color, class, gender, and generation. We need to practice what we preach to bring the kingdom closer, and to free it from the polarizing bonds of free-market or welfare-state partisans playing politics in preachers' clothing.

We need to reach down deep into our own tradition—from class meetings to base communities—and reach across the currents of our own history—from "Amazing Grace" to "Were You There?"—to let the Spirit in and to let it move, to let the Word sing in the souls of the people, and lift them up as the Spirit comes down. That epiphany can take many a graceful form through the heartfelt rhythms of the many-become-one body, keeping together in time, while sparing young and old alike yet another slick seeker service or sappy soft-rock serenade.

Yes, narcississies are the doaters of inversion, and the not-so-new narcissism has grown familiar as an advertising jingle. Yet we can still heed the great majority of Americans, in ranks rising over generations, who say that what matters most to them in life is lifelong love, like Gershwin made clear, a love that is here to stay, not for a year but forever and a day. We can recall with poetic feeling that beauty is momentary in the mind, the fitful tracing of a portal, but in the flesh it is immortal. And where the reverie of a stardust melody from some enchanted evening meets the dawn of each day made new, we can keep the promise of the Word made flesh, and embrace a love that will not fade away, but will be with us always, risen anew among us as members one of another in the Body of Christ.[9]

In our bodies of worship, then, we need to open up the Bible as a

a Soul Mate?" *National Marriage Project: The State of Our Unions, 2001* (Piscataway, NJ: Rutgers University, 2001), 6, 30.

[9] Cf. James Joyce, *Finnegan's Wake* (Oxford: Oxford University Press, 2012), 526; Wallace Stevens, "Peter Quince at the Clavier," *The Collected Poems of Wallace Stevens* (New York: Alfred A. Knopf, 1965), 91; George and Ira Gershwin, "Our Love is Here to Stay"; World Values Survey, U.S. Version, 2000; General Social Survey: Cumulative Datafile, 1972–2012, nos. 480–87, 560–61, 946–50, 1016; Pew Research Center, "Love and Marriage" (2013), available online at http://www.pewforum.org/datasets/faith-in-flux-changes-in-religious-affiliation-in-the-u-s/.

living document, not only to read the words but to sing them, chant them, act them out with Pentecostal fervor and live them out with Social Gospel flair, as Word made flesh and infused with the Holy Spirit in communities of care. This means opening our doors wider to young adults on their own looking for love and companionship, not only to those already married with little children to lead them back to the fold of Sunday school. We need to open up to young and not-so-young singles in twenty-hood and thirty-hood, hungry for communion they can count on in a social world of maximum mobility and uncertainty, driven by the rising costs of middle-class schooling and careers, and buffeted by the rising winds of contingent courtship and marriage coming later in life and less often for keeps.

Those in their twenties and thirties now number one of every two American adults, and they are now deciding the future of our country, and our church, by deciding whether and when to marry or have children, where to live and work and pray. Let's give them all the heedful help, caring communion, and faithful practice that they need. Let's not forget them once youth groups end and campus ministries give way, just as questions of love, work, money, and meaning in the wider world grow more pressing and profound.

And let's ask more of their parents in retirement—one-third of all American adults, and more educated and active than any seniors before them. Let's ask for all they can give to their church and community, which have given so much to them. If we dare to ask like it matters and we mean it, we can also do so much more with them to open our eyes and hearts to the goodness of the world around us, and its neediness, too.

This means opening our arms wider to all those pushed down and pushed apart by the economic hardship that has spread over the past generation. It means heeding parents without partners, workers without jobs, earners without living wages, seniors without caregivers, and spouses without marriage equality. It means heeding our biblical neighbors without a home or a table to share, a voice to raise, or a vote to count.

To tell the truth, eleven o'clock on Sunday morning is still a color-coded hour of the week, and local neighborhoods have grown more economically segregated than before. But communities of faith in America, including our own, are among the least class-divided communities of moral formation, reflection, witness, and inspiration in our society today. Let's give them our all, and make the most of them.

That was then, and this is now. And now, more than ever, an unjust and warring world needs us to live out the unity that Wesley preached two centuries ago:

> If thine heart is as mine, if thou lovest God and all mankind, I ask no more: Give me thine hand. . . . Love me with a very tender affection, as a friend that is closer than a brother; as a brother in Christ, a fellow citizen of the New Jerusalem.[10]

Sisters and brothers—and fellow citizens, too—let us thank God for our blessings, and for the love and labor of our forebears, over a century and more, which have brought us here today. For it is the hands of others that lift us from the womb and lower us to the grave, that bring us aid in our labor, joy in our affection, and consolation in our sorrow.

In this new century, then, let us give our hands to each other, open our arms to our neighbors, and our doors to the world. Let us reach out to touch the heart of humankind. Let us say yes to God's love and justice, here and now in light of the kingdom to come, and let us glorify God in the all-embracing spirit of the church universal, in the communion of all souls, world without end.

---

[10] John Wesley, Sermon 39, "Catholic Spirit" (1750), in *The Works of John Wesley*, vol. 2, *Sermons II (34–70)*, ed. Albert C. Outler (Nashville: Abingdon Press, 1985), 90–92.

Chapter 7

Meeting the Theological Challenges of the New Century

Luke Timothy Johnson

Centennial Academic Conference Keynote Lecture
March 18, 2015

If we ask what the task of theology is within the life of the church and in service to the world, several answers are possible and legitimate. Theology can be thought of alternatively as catechesis or criticism or doxology, depending on whether we see its goal as the handing on of tradition, the assessment of thought and practice, or the praise of God. For a school of theology like Candler, theological education can correspondingly be thought of as equipping students to faithfully transmit the teaching of the church or as distancing students from an unthinking acceptance of traditional ways or as preparing them for a richer experience of worship. All these modes are actively present in our pedagogy.

But another way of construing theology is as a form of prophecy. By prophecy I do not mean the ability to predict the future. I speak of prophecy in biblical terms, as discerning in the complex circumstances of everyday life a Word from God, and speaking that Word to a world that most desperately needs to hear it.

Theology understood as prophecy is a risky proposition. Risky first of all because prophecy seeks to discovery the ways of the living God, and as Hebrews reminds us, it is a terrible thing to fall into the hands of the living God. Risky also, because God's work in the world, here and now, is disclosed only partially, indirectly, and often, darkly.

It is risky above all, though, because the theologian as prophet does not stand above or apart from the context of ordinary life but stands solidly within life as shared by all. The theologian is therefore required to discern and declare God's Word both with boldness and with humility: boldness because the word must be spoken: without a vision the people perish; humility because the theologian holds no position greater than that of servant, wields no power other than that of the word itself.

For a school of theology like Candler, construing theology as prophecy means committing faculty and students alike to the dangerous and exhilarating challenge of moving beyond the exegeting of ancient texts, although that sort of decipherment is always required, to the exegeting of the complex and ever-changing texts of worldly life. We seek to learn how to hear and to speak the Word that is God's own amid the constant noise and distraction of human babble. Students and faculty together desire learning how to think on their feet, speak to the point, and bear witness passionately. We must together embrace the risk of engaging God's world directly and without safety goggles.

Theology as Prophecy

This conference on the occasion of Candler's centennial represents just such an effort to do theology in a prophetic mode. We have gathered ourselves together with friends and respected peers, not to deliver academic papers that may or may not find their way into a learned volume, but to speak simply and candidly, to listen carefully and respectfully, and to discuss responsibly some of the great theological challenges that face all of us, as we move into this school's second hundred years. We do not pretend to be prophets in the predictive sense: we have no special ability to foretell the future. We take on only the daunting task of discerning what God might be up to in the world now, and to what response God might be calling us as disciples of the Lord Jesus Christ.

To expect those who founded this school one hundred years ago to be prophetic in any sense of the term would have been fatuous, much like expecting the Pilgrims in 1620 to step off the *Mayflower* onto Plymouth Rock and immediately declare America's foreign policy. In 1914, Atlanta was quite literally making the turn from horse and carriage to automobile; how could anyone then living predict the technological revolutions that would transform every aspect of life: the air conditioning that would change the old to the new South, the antibiotics that would conquer infections and extend life, the cybernetics that would change communication and even consciousness, the planes that would span the globe and the rockets that would leap to space?

Who in 1914 Atlanta could have predicted that the great European empires would dissolve, that colonialism would disappear, that new world powers would emerge from the Far East, that Africa would be the arena for great adventures in suppression and liberation, that the combination of mineral resources and religious upheaval would make Islamic lands have an importance greater than at any time in history? How could anyone imagine that the great war of 1914 would initiate a century of warfare in which advanced technology would be employed for the slaughter of untold millions? Who in the Edwardian age could have dreamed that humans would be capable of ideologically inspired genocide on the scale of the Shoah in Nazi German or the Gulag Archipelago of Stalin or the killing fields of Pol Pot?

In 1914, even the great theological centers of Europe showed themselves unaware of the cataclysmic events that the twentieth century would bring, and ill-equipped to respond to them when they occurred. Theological responses to war and genocide and social oppression in the twentieth century tended to be weak and late. No surprise, then, that the founders of Candler, with a tiny faculty and few students and truly meager resources, would have kept their eyes fixed mainly on the catechetical and doxological dimensions of theology as they sought to form ministers for the Methodist Episcopal Church, South.

Mainly, but not entirely. In the great battle between fundamentalism and modernism that has dominated American theology from the time of Candler's founding, this school aligned itself quickly and consistently with modernism. The reputation of being "liberal," that is, of encouraging and supporting free inquiry into Scripture and Tradition has been Candler's throughout its history, most famously in the "Death of God" controversy, with not always positive consequences for the perception of the school in a predominantly conservative region and church. In similar fashion, although Candler as an institution was agonizingly slow to advance the cause of racial equality, its first professor of New Testament wrote passionately against racist practices and Candler's alumni were among the most prominent figures in raising regional consciousness on the issue. Andrew Sledd in practice anticipated a disposition that Hendrikus Boers, a later Candler New Testament professor, described as "bringing theology out of the ghetto" of ecclesiastical self-grooming.

Theological Issues Facing Us Today

We seek in this conference to stand within that Candler tradition of free inquiry and of passion for social justice. We attempt to do theology in a prophetic mode, by considering together four issues, which in our judgment demand our best attention now, and will, in all likelihood, continue to demand the attention of theologians through the coming century: theological imagination and secularization; the image of God in contemporary society; creation and the care of the earth; and, the kingdom of God and global pluralism.

The four topics have, in turn, five characteristics in common that recommend them particularly to our attention today. First, they are all grounded in Scripture and the Creed; they involve convictions close to the core of Christian identity. Second, they have all been the subject of examination in the earlier theological tradition; there are resources from which we can draw. Third, they all involve developments in history and culture, making them especially attractive to this school's habit of practicing theology contextually. Fourth, they all are under serious threat in the contemporary world; they press upon us with particular urgency. Finally, they are topics to which this faculty has devoted and is devoting serious attention; we actually have something to say.

Theological Imagination and Secularization

The first theme we consider is that of the Word of God. No need to defend the centrality of this topic within Christian faith. Scripture declares that God creates the world through speech and communicates with creatures through speech. The medium of God's revelation to humans is the Word, expressed first though inchoately through creation itself, then through God's self-disclosure in law, in prophecy, and in wisdom. God's Word, we confess, is most fully revealed through the incarnation of God's Son Jesus Christ, in his embodied presence among humans, in his scandalous death, and in his glorious exaltation as Lord. Through the presence of God's Holy

Spirit, we also affirm, God's Word continues to be spoken in and through the experiences of men and women. The gift and task of the church, therefore, is to be the place in the world where the Word of God is truly embodied and powerfully expressed, so that the power and presence of God that is only implicitly present within human experience might be brought to full articulation within the community gathered by the Holy Spirit in the name of Jesus. Sacrament and the word of proclamation each witness to realities that are no less real for being unseen.

The theological tradition has naturally devoted sustained attention to the revelatory word, debating the ways by which God's Word in Scripture is best interpreted, inquiring into the adequacy of human speech to express divine mysteries, distinguishing between the orders of natural and supernatural revelation, identifying the ways that God's Word calls humans to the obedience of faith. Until relatively recently, however, preachers of the Word could assume that if the Word was proclaimed clearly and passionately, it would find a hearing in human hearts. A few stones may need to be cleared; the birds and the weeds need to be controlled, but there is always good soil for the seed to take root and grow.

There were always problems posed to effective preaching by cultural diversity, to be sure; thus, the persistent concern to translate the Scriptures into language intelligible to people in diverse settings—if people could only hear of God's wonders in words of their own, they would recognize God's Word and respond to it in faith. But the optimism of Christian preaching was always based on the premise that humans, no matter how alienated their existence or how depraved their behavior, still had a longing for the truth, an instinct for the divine, that enabled them both to hear and obey God's call.

According to this premise, humans have a natural tropism toward God: people seek something beyond the things they touch and taste; they have a longing for something more than the everyday world offers them. Christian preaching historically found success among those who were in one way or another already religious: the poor of the land in Israel, the God-fearers among the Gentiles, Gothic and Celtic worshipers, adherents of tribal cults. The Gospel provided a distinctive and convincing version of a truth that their hearts already sought without knowing. But was that religious instinct solely a matter of the heart's natural longing, or was it also a consequence of cultural formation?

We know that there have always been thoroughly secular people, who defined themselves explicitly by what they saw and touched, and who lived their lives in disregard of the divine. But such folk were historically a tiny minority, and their secular stance was actively discouraged by societies that supported and rewarded religious adherence. Take for example the Greco-Roman culture within which Christianity found its first and most lasting success: skeptics like the Epicureans and thoroughgoing secular types like the heroes of the *Satyrikon* are notable exceptions; the structure of society supported a piety that embraced both politics and religion in a single vision; more important, the form of education (*paideia*) reinforced this vision, so that Greeks and Romans thought naturally in terms of a "city of gods and men."

Today, that historical premise for proclamation is no longer obvious. The challenge facing theology today with respect to God's Word is not disordered religiosity but the apparent absence of religious sensibility in the contemporary First World, an absence carved out of human consciousness in turn by the Enlightenment, by the astounding successes of science and technology, and by powerful ideological forces making the argument, with the ancient Epicureans, that the beginning of human liberation is the banishment of religious piety. Secularity—defining reality solely in terms of matter, seeing the world not as mystery but as a set of interlocking problems and answers—is now no longer the quirk of idiosyncratic individuals or of odd groups. It is the defining element of First World culture, supported and reinforced by politics, commerce, and education.

The theological challenge facing us today is therefore more radical than for the founders of Candler, who could assume in their students and in their congregants both a language and a perception of the world shaped by religious convictions and commitments, who knew that when they spoke of sacrifice for others or of seeking God's will, or of values transcending self-interest, such ideas were already familiar to those culturally shaped by late Christendom. No such assumption can be made today. Today, theology must come to grips with a radical and pervasive secularity that makes speaking of God at all increasingly strange, even quaint. It must come to grips also

with the fact that the effects of secularism affect in profoundly cor-
rupting ways, even those who profess religious belief. The challenge
of how we might speak God's word today is real, is serious, and not
for the weak of heart.

The Image of God in Contemporary Society

The second theological topic we consider in this conference is the
image of God in contemporary society. The conviction that humans
are in fact created in the image of God is one that derives entirely
from Scripture rather than the observation of human behavior. It is a
perfect example of the way Scripture does not so much describe the
world as imagine a world, and invite us, by imagining the world in
the same way, to make it real. We should never have come to such a
perception on our own. As Chesterton famously noted, the only
Christian doctrine that can be empirically verified is that of original
sin. But we are schooled by Scripture to regard ourselves and every
other human as bearing the impress of the divine; indeed, because of
Jesus' exaltation as life-giving Spirit (1 Cor 15:45), Saint Paul insists,
we are to imagine ourselves and other people as bearing the image
of Christ as well: "just as we have borne the image of the man of
dust," Paul tells us, "we will also bear the image of the man of heaven"
(1 Cor 15:49).

Christian theological anthropology is thus inherently complex
and tension-filled. On one side, Scripture proposes a truth about
ourselves that we could never imagine on our own; on the other side,
Scripture also instructs us to pay the closest attention to our actual
mortal bodies, for through them we find God's spirit disclosed in the
world. Not only changes in human consciousness, then, but also
changes in human bodies are significant for thinking about the image of God. Today, the digital revolution is, with unparalleled speed,
changing our culture and promises to alter even the structures of human consciousness. Medical technology, in turn, has increased lon-
gevity and enabled an astonishing range of physical alterations:
organ transplants, prostheses, plastic surgery, transgendering, clon-
ing—all these transmogrifications press on us serious reflection on
what human identity might mean in the face of such malleability.
What might it mean to be created in the image of God when we or
our neighbors are cyborgs?

71

Speaking of the neighbor, our convictions concerning God's impress on humans demands that we think in moral as well as ontological terms. Scripture's language, in fact, tends to focus on the imperative to treat humans differently because they are stamped with God's image. The third statement of it in Genesis 9:6 declares, "Whoever sheds the blood of a human by a human shall that person's blood be shed, for in his own image God made humankind," and the last in James 3:9 decries the evil use of the tongue, "with it we bless the Lord and Father, and with it we curse those who are made in the likeness of God." Paul similarly links bearing the image of Christ and the way we treat others: "When you sin against the brothers, and wound their weak conscience, you sin against Christ" (1 Cor 8:12). The dignity, even the sacrality, of human life, and the basis for all claims to religious and other rights, is located in the special character of the human person as created in God's image: how we treat our neighbor is the measure of our response to God.

The historical record reaching from Cain and Abel to the killing fields of Ruwanda, however, does not suggest that this doctrine has had much of a positive influence on human relations; the tale of human savagery and violence is both long and dismal. People have been conquering each other in war, have raped and pillaged, have taken into captivity, have degraded and mocked other people, apparently as long as they have been aware of each other. But it can legitimately be asked whether over the hundred years since Candler was founded, the pitch and pace of human savagery has not made both a quantitative and qualitative leap, in part at least to the very processes of secularization that I spoke of earlier. It may be, in fact, that this past century has seen an unprecedented convergence of human cruelty, technological capacity, and ideological justification, leading to forms of genocide, enslavement, discrimination, and degradation that former ages could scarcely have imagined, and which makes any effort to think creatively about the human person a perilous proposition. Recovering some sense of this most fragile and precious of theological convictions is difficult, not least because of the overwhelming amount of experience that seems to contradict it. As Gerard Manley Hopkins lamented concerning God's grandeur,

Generations have trod, have trod, have trod;
   And all is seared with trade; bleared, smeared with toil;
   And wears man's smudge and shares man's smell: the soil
Is bare now, nor can foot feel, being shod."[1]

It is difficult, but it is also necessary directly in proportion to its difficulty.

Creation and Care of the Earth

That frightening quotation from Hopkins can serve as a transition to our third theological topic, creation and the care of the earth. The crisis of the present moment can be seen as shaped by the collision of two realities. The first is the recognition that Christians have participated in practices deriving from a distorted vision of the human place in God's creation. The second is the sudden and shocking realization that such practices threaten to damage or even destroy the work of God in creation. Candler's founders had no sense of the issue: the term "ecology" was only coined in 1873, and began to be used for human interactions with the environment in the 1960s. But now, it forms a major dimension of our awareness of the world.

The distorted Christian vision of humanity's place in the cosmos has taken two main forms. The first derives from the powerful dualistic view of the world that we associate in its mild form with Christian Platonism and in its severe form with Gnosticism: matter is at best a shell for the spirit and at worst a prison; the point of human existence is to liberate the soul from the body. In this construction, the notion of "caring for the earth" is a form of entanglement of that deceptive materiality from which the soul ought to flee. A more contemporary form of such dualism is the fervent expectation of the rescue of the elect from the spaceship earth where they have been trapped, with their being swept up to heaven, leaving "the late great planet earth" to conflagration and destruction.

If the Gnostic version saw only the soul worth saving and regarded all other creatures with at best benign neglect, a second theological position—this one based squarely on a certain understanding of humans being created in the image of God—adopted a far more aggressive stance toward creatures regarded as

---

[1] Gerard Manley Hopkins, "God's Grandeur," in *Gerard Manley Hopkins: Poems and Prose* (London: Penguin Books, 1985), 27.

73

lower links on the great chain of being. The scriptural warrant for such a sense of superiority is clear enough. Having created male and female in God's image, "God blessed them, and God said to them, 'Be fruitful and multiply, and fill the earth and subdue it; and have dominion over the fish of the sea and over the birds of the air and over every living thing that moves upon the earth'" (Gen 1:28). This majestic imperative has historically overshadowed the humbler but now suddenly more persuasive scene where "The Lord God took the man and put him in the garden of Eden to till it and to keep it," and placed strict boundaries to the human exploitation of the garden's fruits (Gen 2:15-17).

Ecological blindness is not entirely the fault of the Bible or Christian theology. Christians lived for centuries with these or similar views in remarkable harmony with other creatures. The Rule of Benedict, for example, instructed monks to view the land and the tools with which they worked as they did the vessels of the altar, inculcating a pervasive sense of piety toward material things as well as the soul. Such monastic virtue was in fact formerly blamed for the world's failure to develop itself technologically and for humanity's failure to realize its Promethean ambition.

Indeed, material exploitation and despoliation are far more the result of attitudes and practices that have developed in direct opposition to classical Christian tenets. It is the spirit of the Enlightenment, after all, that seeks to demystify everything, reduce mystery to problem, magic to statistics. Cartesian dualism did more than Christian mysticism to cultivate the perception of the body as a machine and the world as the mind's laboratory. Above all, it has been the spirit of capitalism—fundamentally in tension with the Christian ideal of sharing possessions—that has fostered competitive acquisition as the measure of human success, and has succeeded in reducing all things material and spiritual to marketplace commodities.

More than anything else, the effects of technological revolution—and the human population explosion such technology supports—have fundamentally altered the relation between humans and the rest of creation. The impact of our insatiable growth and consumption have on the survivability, not only of every other species, but (to speak in the most selfish way possible) of the human species as well is something we are still struggling to comprehend. The impact could not have been understood even a hundred years

ago, when the consequences of the human drive for power, possessions and pleasure, abetted by mind-boggling technological prowess, and multiplied by swarming populations, could not yet even be
imagined. Nature still seemed then, even for one as far-sighted as
Theodore Roosevelt, to be infinitely vast, infinitely rich and varied
in life and resource, even infinitely frightening when compared to
human strength and cunning. We could not yet then leap into space,
and look down on our beloved planet and see it as a stunningly
beautiful yet suddenly fragile blue marble. But now we have so seen
it, and that makes all the difference.

Putting aside the question of blame, there are three reasons why
Christians now bear a distinctive responsibility for responding to
the ecological crisis. First, there are more Christians in the world
than adherents of any other religion; what Christians think and do
matters. Second, of all the world's religions, Christianity has been
uniquely corrupted by the spirit of modernity, that combination of
Enlightenment reason, technology, individualism, commodification,
and consumerism; conversion is called for. Third, Christianity is the
dominant religion in the parts of the world most responsible for the
despoliation of the earth's resources; because of their privileged position, the conversion of Christians is the most important and can
have the greatest impact.

Conversion is not a matter of making apologies or of engaging in
symbolic protests or of each of us doing our bit by recycling. The
change required is massive. It requires a change of mind as well as of
the heart. And this is precisely the theological challenge: to think of
God's creation and of the relation of humans to other creatures in
ways that restore the sense of wonder and reverence at God's work,
that leads to a sense of appreciation for the equality and necessary
reciprocity among all beings, that yields dispositions and practices
that are more profoundly in accord with God's vision for the world.
It is a challenge we might not have chosen, but it is one we must
engage, for the stakes could not be higher.

The Kingdom of God and Global Pluralism

The final issue we address in this conference again demands the
reassessment of traditional teaching in light of contemporary circumstances. In this case it is the conviction, rooted in the preaching

of Jesus himself, that God is king of the universe and, as Jesus expressed in his prayer, that God desires his will to be done on earth as it is in heaven. In Paul's first letter to the Corinthians, a corollary of Jesus' exaltation to God's right hand is that Christ rules over all cosmic powers until he in turn hands over final sovereignty to God, so that God will be "all things in all things." The Nicene Creed declares as the hope of the Christian people the expectation of a kingdom that shall never end.

But convictions concerning the kingdom of God—even among those little bothered by the hegemonic or patriarchal implications of the language—have never been easy to correlate with conditions on the ground. Christians from the beginning experienced a tension between the already and not yet of God's dominion, with believers locating themselves either primarily (and optimistically) in terms of God's presence now or (more pessimistically) in terms of God's triumph in the future. There was also the question of the relationship of God's rule to human kingdoms. With Constantine's establishment of Christianity as the religion of the empire, the church began a misalliance with human political power that lasted until very recently, and that made it seem fitting to wed evangelism to colonialism. Only with the hammer blows to religion's establishment struck by political revolution in the United States, France, and Russia, has the church found itself largely unsupported by civil government and able at last to embrace the diaspora awareness that was natural to it in the first four centuries of its existence.

Despite such uncertainties, Christian theologians have always been serenely confident about declaring who was to be included and who excluded from God's rule, or to put it more precisely, who would experience that rule positively as salvation and who as damnation. Outside the church, the slogan said, there is no salvation. A great deal of Christian self-definition over the centuries—involving an astonishing amount of intellectual passion and energy—has consequently been devoted to deciding issues of inclusion and exclusion, always to the advantage, to be sure, of those doing the deciding. From the start, authentic belief was defined in terms of an absolute either/or, and located in contrast to rival seekers after God: among the Gentiles, there could be only darkness, no light; among the Jews, there could be only blindness, not sight. The practice of Gentile religion was demonic; the practice of Judaism was stubborn disobedience. A massive amount of Christian theology from the first is systemically anti-Gentile, and profoundly supersesssionist with respect to Judaism.

Defining by exclusion continues in the long tradition of heresiology: getting anything wrong means getting everything wrong, means falling outside the realm of God's rule. In a time of relatively robust ecumenism among families of Christians today, it is helpful to remember that in the time of Candler's founding, scurrilous attacks between Catholics and Protestants were standard fare, and missions to Africa were regarded in terms of an urgent rescue of pagan babies from the clutch of demons, and theological Jew-baiting was common in Christian sermons.

All of this theological map-making was carried out with supreme indifference to what might actually be happening—still less what God might be up to—among Jews and the countless Gentiles who had never heard of Jesus or perhaps had never heard of him apart from the sinister implications of Western imperialism.

Christian theologians were like pre-Copernican astronomers who could draw exquisite charts of the stars and planets visible to those resting comfortably on the planet they complacently assumed was the center of the universe. The past hundred years have rudely jerked us from that state of complacency to a lonelier and more isolated place in a Copernican universe. The tragedy of the holocaust has revealed the rot that lay at the center of Christian supersessionism, and forces us to ask what gift it is we celebrate as Christians when we no longer define it as "not Judaism." The collapse of colonialism has revealed how corrupt the alliance between Christian mission and Western political ambition truly was. Islam has awakened from its centuries-long slumber to become the fastest growing religion on the planet, making claims concerning God's rule and its connection to the state that are eerily reminiscent of Christianity's Constantinian dalliance. The Gentile religions of the present—above all those of India and China—are not long ago and far away, but in our schools and playgrounds. The secularization of the so-called First World has revealed the powerful ideological forces that not only diminish the role of Christianity in society but challenge the default premise favoring religion. In short, Christians and Christian theology must today come to grips with a pluralism that is both global and radical.

On this topic, we truly are at the starting point. With regard to the question of the church and the world, we need to start over. The task is massive and demanding. We are not sure how to reread Scripture and the tradition with sufficiently fresh eyes. But at stake is the authenticity and integrity of Christian preaching within a world that truly is under God's rule rather than ours.

Conclusion

These, then, are the theological themes that we seek to address in this centennial academic conference. Let me conclude this presentation by anticipating three objections to the agenda we have set.

First, our selection of topics omits issues of arguably even greater urgency and even greater visibility. Why not speak prophetically to the issue of ecumenism and church unity, of the historical Jesus, or of the prosperity Gospel, or the persistent conflict among Christians between fundamentalist and modernist? While not denying the importance of taking a stance on each of these issues, they are not of such fundamental importance, for the world as well as for the church, as the themes we have chosen.

Second, it may be objected that the topics we have selected are insufficiently theological, in the sense that they do not derive directly from the church's confession or lead directly to prayer and piety. They tilt rather to cultural analysis and ethics. They are perhaps too much critical and not enough doxological. Our answer to this objection is simply that this is the way we do theology here at Candler. Over the several decades that we have tried to learn and to teach each other how to think theologically within social and pastoral contexts, we have now become unable to think of theology as a subject that ever lacks cultural dimensions and ethical entailments. And, we are convinced that this is just the sort of theology of which our world is most in need.

Finally, each of these themes taken by itself could command the attention of many such conferences. We are well aware that taking them on all together this way in such a short span of time can make our treatment appear to be introductory and superficial. It is our hope, though, that our conversation will bring to light other dimensions of each topic, and that by putting all these topics into play at one time, we can appreciate the interconnections among them. We do not pretend to know ahead of time how our theological conversation will turn out. But we do not intend to close a conversation. We want to start a conversation that can help shape the next hundred years of this school and be a prophetic voice for the church and world.

CHAPTER 8

"Great Birds of the Kingdom": Theological Imagination and Secularization

Ted A. Smith

Centennial Academic Conference Lecture
March 19, 2015

The language of "secularization" is often used to describe a process that happens outside the walls of the church. Secularization is seen as an external, alien force that pushes those walls in, shrinking the space in which the church can flourish and the kinds of influence it can exert. I want to set that sense of secularization aside for the time being, neither affirming it nor rejecting it. I want to focus instead on dynamics that happen within the walls of churches and even within core practices of church life. More specifically, I want to consider how secularization happens within the practice of telling stories in sermons.

These dynamics are visible in a sermon story told just about one hundred years ago by a Methodist Bishop named Warren Akin Candler. There is irony in any story that describes Bishop Candler as contributing to a process of secularization. That certainly wasn't his intention. But we preachers are always doing more than we know, more than we intend. There is judgment in that. And there is grace.

Warren Akin Candler did all that he could as a church leader in the late nineteenth and early twentieth century to resist what he saw as forces of secularization. Institutionally, he worked in his role as first chancellor of the modern version of Emory University to forge unbreakable legal bonds between the university and the Methodist Episcopal Church, South. Theologically, he opposed what he called the "soup and soap" religion of the Social Gospel. Instead he proclaimed what he and his hearers thought of as an old-time religion stressing personal salvation. He was by all accounts a powerhouse of a preacher. Once in Alabama, the story goes, he preached with such warmth and conviction that even Presbyterians— Presbyterians!—walked across the tops of pews to come forward when he called them to the altar.

The content and the intention of Bishop's Candler's sermons resisted secularization in every way. But the form of his preaching— and especially the way in which he told stories—reflected and deepened the worldview in which an emerging secularity flourished. "Secularity" can mean many things. Here I do not mean that Bishop Candler's preaching produced a decline in religious belief or practice. On the contrary, he seems to have brought many people into greater participation in church life. And I do not mean to say that he contributed to the differentiation of a religious sphere from other spheres of society. On the contrary, he fought fiercely for tax exemption for church-related colleges and universities on the grounds that their work was continuous with the larger mission of the nation. What I do mean to say is this: Candler's style of telling sermon stories fit with a way of seeing the world as if it had no theological significance except what an individual person imposed upon it. In this Candler was far from alone. He told sermon stories like almost every other white Protestant preacher in his day—and ours. This way of telling stories both reflected and deepened the hold of what Charles Taylor has called the background beliefs of a secular age.[1]

Candler would never have consciously assented to those beliefs. But they shaped what he counted as plausible. They shaped what made sense. And so they shaped the kinds of sense he made. Consider the story Candler told in a sermon entitled "The Church of Jesus Christ":

Do you remember the story of Columbus starting out to discover a new world in little frail Spanish caravels? Without a

---

[1] Charles Taylor, *A Secular Age* (Cambridge: Harvard University Press, 2007), 13–14.

chart he sailed the seas, as thoroughly derided as sceptical men deride the future life. On and on and on he sailed until the sailors with him grew doubtful and mutinous and were ready to throw him overboard and retrace their way back to Spain. But as the old mariner walked the deck in anxiety, the land birds came soaring about the sails, and the fruits of the land were floating on the waters while yet the shore line could not be discerned; and he raised the jubilant cry, "This is land ahead!" And every sailor was out of his hammock, and joyous chorus broke over those silent seas, "Land ahead!" And there was land ahead! So our mutinous souls, often despondent and anxious for the Church, are sailing over uncharted waters through months and days and years. And we grow fearful and disquieted. But betimes the fruits of the Spirit come floating on the bosom of the deep, and the great birds of the kingdom come singing in the sails, and we begin to cry out, "Land ahead!" And, blessed be God, there is land ahead! "Christ in you the hope of glory."[2]

Candler used the story of the land birds to illustrate his point that God sends signs of hope when we need them. Truth resided in the point, which took the form of a general claim that stood above history and applied equally to every moment in history: God sends signs of hope. The story of the birds illustrated this point. And it illustrated the point because Candler decided to use it in this way. There was nothing in the story itself that was integrally connected to the point before Candler made the connection for his hearers. Because all the theological significance resided in the point, and because the story connected to the point only as Candler made the connection, Candler preached as if the events of the story had no theological significance in themselves.

Because the events did not carry theological significance in themselves, it did not matter to Candler if things happened exactly the way he said they did on the decks of the *Niña*, the *Pinta*, and the *Santa María*. Candler could feel free — even obliged — to make up the details that made the story come to life: Columbus pacing the deck, the sailors in their hammocks, the scraps of dialogue. Within the conventions of this kind of sermon story, Candler did nothing wrong in presenting these inventions as if they described the way

[2] Warren Akin Candler, "The Church of Jesus Christ," Warren A. Candler Papers, Stuart A. Rose Manuscript, Archives, and Rare Book Library, Emory University.

things actually happened. For the truth of the story depended not on the details of the narrative, but on the point which it illustrated. It did not matter if there were no hammocks on the *Santa María* (and, in fact, there weren't—Columbus and his crew "discovered" hammocks when they saw them being used by the people they called Indians). The empirical accuracy of such details is irrelevant in this kind of story. The story could be fiction, or even fiction presented as if it were fact, as these stories often were and are. For the measure that this kind of sermon story sets for itself is not its *correspondence* to what happened in 1492, but its *effectiveness* in illustrating a theological claim that applies equally to every time and place.

This practice of telling stories as illustrations reflected and contributed to a worldview in which a kind of secularity flourished. Whatever the conscious intentions of the preacher, the practice of telling stories as illustrations projected a world in which theological truths existed on a different order from historical narratives. The truth of God was not in the story, not in history. Any connections between the story and the truth were created—not found—by the preacher. If the sensible world acquired theological significance, it was because of the actions of an individual person. And the chief criterion for evaluating a person's work in making that connection was its usefulness for persuading other people of a truth above history. The assumptions embedded in this practice reinforced a way of seeing in which individual subjects make whatever meaning there is in the world. They also fit with a centuries-long expansion of instrumental reason that values usefulness more than qualities like beauty or accuracy. And they reflect a vision in which knowledge is divided between an idealist theology that never quite touches the ground and an empiricist account of the world that operates entirely within an immanent network of causes and effects. They fit with a secular age.

This way of telling stories still reflects and shapes the background beliefs of our age. The form of narrative illustration and theological point is common to many different styles and traditions of preaching. The steady publication of collections of illustrative stories and now video clips suggests just how common the practice has become. The practice fits with more than just our preaching, though. It fits with the ways we organize knowledge. In particular, it fits with the ways we divide empirical from moral or theological ways of knowing. This division shapes everything from elementary-school instruction in the difference between "fact" and "opinion" to the structure of a university in which the natural and social sciences stand on one side while the humanities stand on the other—and theology stands in the farthest corner of humanities. Lessing's ditch remains deep and wide. It is one of the boundaries that orders our world.

These boundaries and the illustrative stories that fit within them are so familiar that it can be difficult to see what is at stake in the practice—or even that we are engaged in a particular practice at all. The practice comes into sharper focus when we remember some of the ways of telling stories that it displaced. Let me remember just one of them today.

The Puritans who preached two and three centuries before Bishop Candler made extensive use of *typological* stories.[3] In telling these stories they drew upon centuries of Jewish and Christian typology. These traditions paired a "type"—some thing, person, or event—with an "antitype" that represented its fulfillment. In his letter to the church in Rome, for example, the apostle Paul called Adam a "type" of Christ (Adam the type prefigured Christ the antitype) (Rom 5:14). Later generations of Christian interpreters seized hold of the Gospels' talk of a "sign of Jonah" to read Jonah as another type of Christ: Jonah's three days in the belly of the whale anticipated Jesus' own three-day journey through death to new life. Still other interpreters expanded typology beyond Scripture to all of history. Persons or events in this age could be read as types that would be fulfilled in the age to come.

Puritan preachers adapted typological traditions even as they criticized what they saw as the excesses of late medieval and early modern rhetoric. To Puritan critics, the worst excesses arose when preachers relied too much on rhetoric and not enough on logic (or "dialectic"). Puritan "plain-style" preachers made a sharp distinction

---

[3] For a more complete discussion of the shift from the typological stories of Puritans to the illustrative stories of revival preachers, see Ted A. Smith, *The New Measures: A Theological History of Democratic Practice* (Cambridge: Cambridge University Press, 2007), 223–30.

between logic and rhetoric. The relevant difference was this: logic was given, built into the order of things by God, while rhetoric was made, a product of human innovation. To trust too much in rhetoric, then, was to trust too much in one's own powers. And so the plain-style preachers were suspicious of what they saw as fanciful allegories and glittering literary devices.

But still they told stories. Some of these stories they allowed themselves as guilty rhetorical pleasures. But the most important stories plain-style preachers told did not count as "rhetoric" at all, for they depended on typological connections between the age described in the story and the age in which the story was fulfilled. Such stories counted as logic for plain-style preachers because they worked through connections that were found, not made, by the preacher. Those connections existed to be found, plain-style preachers held, because God had established them out of God's gracious desire to be known. And so the stories counted as logic. As logic, these typological stories could provide the substance of the sermon, not just a spoonful of narrative sugar to help the doctrine go down. They could be used without risk of excess. And so typological stories of many kinds flourished in Puritan preaching. Typology was central to the occasional sermons through which Puritan preachers interpreted the lives of their communities. An analogous typological imagination informed the testimonies of individual believers, both men and women, who described the observable events of their lives as divinely ordained signs of God's electing grace.

The background beliefs that could sustain such typological visions were already waning when Jonathan Edwards was born in 1703. But Edwards displayed a typological vision that was as rich as any that we know. For much of his life he kept a volume he called "Images of Divine Things" in which he recorded observations of a natural world full of types that pointed to the sovereign grace of God. Theology *had* to work in this way, Edwards thought, because of the nature of language. Edwards believed that the origin of every word was in the experience of some sensible quality. I touch an ice cube; I have an experience; I need a word for what I experience; I say "cold." But if words came from empirical experience, how could we ever talk about things that we do not touch, taste, see, hear or feel — things like theology, or morality? We could talk about morality and theology, Edwards wrote, only because God had created analogies that allowed things we *could* see, touch, taste, hear and feel to "shadow forth, picture or image" things beyond our senses.[4] "The works of God are but a kind of voice or language of God," Edwards wrote, "to instruct intelligent beings in things pertaining to himself."[5] The very possibility of talking about God or goodness depended upon this typological connection between sensible events and theological truths.

This mode of revelation was not a grudging accommodation of human frailty, in Edwards's eyes. On the contrary, it was, he wrote, "very fit and becoming of God." For God established typological connections—God made the things of this age an alphabet of glory—not just because fallen humans needed them, but because it delighted God to work in this way.

With this vision, the whole world came alive to Edwards as shadows of divine love. Natural phenomena did not serve, he wrote, "merely . . . as illustrations of [God's] meaning, but as illustrations and evidences of the truth of what he says."[6] They functioned not as illustrative examples of general truths but as typological images of particular promises. Edwards saw these typological connections everywhere. He saw shadows of divine things in the way a snake caught its prey, the experience of climbing a hill, the waves of a stormy sea, the stench of a corpse, and the habit of taking off one's clothes before sleeping. Even the silkworm, in Edwards's eyes, was "a remarkable type of Christ." It dies as a worm, as Christ died in the

---

[4] Edwards is quoting George Turnbull. Jonathan Edwards, "Images of Divine Things," in *The Works of Jonathan Edwards*, vol. 11, *Typological Writings*, ed. Wallace E. Anderson, et al., (New Haven: Yale University Press, 1993), 125–26. Turnbull's account of language owes much to John Locke. See John Locke, *An Essay Concerning Human Understanding*, ed. Peter Nidditch (Oxford: Oxford University Press, 1975), §III.ii.1. On "Images of Divine Things" and the broader question of Edwards and typology, see Wallace E. Anderson, "Editor's Introduction to 'Images of Divine Things' and 'Types'," in *The Works of Jonathan Edwards*, vol. 11, *Typological Writings*, and Wilson H. Kimnach, "General Introduction to the Sermons: Jonathan Edwards' Art of Prophesying," in *The Works of Jonathan Edwards*, vol. 10, *Sermons and Discourses, 1720–1723*, ed. Wilson H. Kimnach (New Haven: Yale University Press, 1992), esp. 6–9, 186, 99, 210ff.

[5] Edwards, "Images of Divine Things," in *The Works of Jonathan Edwards*, vol. 11, *Typological Writings*, ed. Anderson, et al., 67.

[6] Ibid., 57.

state of his humiliation, but then rises to new life as a more glorious creature in the butterfly. And it leaves behind silk that becomes for us beautiful clothing, just as Christ's death weaves for us the glorious clothing in which we are justified before God.[7] Edwards's silkworm did not merely illustrate an abstract claim about imputed grace. It revealed the nature of grace in the way that it pleased God to make God's ways known. And because God chose to communicate in this way, even the smallest empirical details of the story mattered.

Edwards the preacher and mystic saw the world typologically, but Edwards the pastor and college president knew that few people in his day would agree with him. "I expect by very ridicule and contempt to be called a man of a very fruitful brain and copious fancy," he wrote.[8] He kept his typological thoughts to himself. The notebooks were not published until they became interesting as historical artifacts more than two hundred years later.

As Edwards anticipated, the divinely ordained types of Puritans became less and less plausible over the course of the eighteenth century. The expansion of religious pluralism, migration between and within countries, belief that people could shape their own destinies, and the power of science to explain the world within an immanent frame all eroded confidence in such typologies. In the nineteenth century some white Protestant preachers and politicians still told typological jeremiads about church or national identity. A few virtuosi like Herman Melville gathered the embers of typological consciousness to light new kinds of fires. Most Catholic and African American preachers continued to use at least some typology that presumed divinely established connections between earthly and heavenly realities. In the early twentieth century Pentecostals would revive this practice again. But for most of the people and institutions in the lines that connected Edwards to Candler, divinely ordained typology stopped making sense.

The shift in sermon stories from type to illustration registers a host of changes in the forms of life that prevailed in the time of Edwards

---

[7] Ibid., 100.
[8] Ibid,. 152.

compared to those that prevailed in the time of Candler. The story of this journey from Edwards's typological silkworm to Candler's illustrative birds is the story of a kind of disenchantment. It is tempting for those of us who care about theology to tell a story of disenchantment as a narrative of decline. American churches are full of such narratives today.

I want to resist that temptation, though, and for three reasons. First, it suggests a remedy that does not take seriously our lives as finite creatures in time (a truth Edwards himself would not let us forget). A narrative of decline can stir in us the desire to restore what we have lost, to spin again stories in which we could receive the silkworm as a type of Christ. But we cannot restore a typological imagination by fiat or social reform, even if we want to. We cannot undo the deep shifts of many centuries simply by changing the way we tell sermon stories. There is something self-defeating in the effort. For if the problem is our knowledge of our role in making meaning, then we cannot solve that problem through our efforts to make the world a more meaningful sort of place. We can't pull ourselves up into Edwards's typological vision by our own theological bootstraps.

Second, a simple narrative of decline would leave out the real goods that came with the move from type to illustration. These include not just the fruits of a scientific worldview, which are real enough, however mixed the uses to which we turn them, but also an ethos of equality that arose hand-in-hand with the move from types to illustrations. Elsewhere I have argued that Alexis de Tocqueville saw this connection clearly.[9] Tocqueville visited the United States just at the time when revival preachers were casting off typological stories for illustrations of general points. He saw the fit between an emphasis on equality and the tendency to reason with general principles. People who live in aristocratic societies, Tocqueville wrote, tend to avoid general categories for interpreting the world and the place of people in it. A category like "citizen" has little purchase. The world is understood instead through particular names, like Louis XIV. But the person who lives in a democracy "cannot consider any part whatsoever of the human species without having his thought enlarge and dilate to embrace the sun. All truths applicable to himself appear to him to apply equally and in the same manner to each

---

[9] Smith, *The New Measures*, 237–38.

of his fellow citizens and to those like him."[10] Typological stories fit with an old world in which some were elect and others were not and in which some were noble and others were not. But stories that illustrated general truths fit with a church that offered salvation to whosoever would accept it and with a polity that promised equal rights to every citizen. If the promises of that polity have not been perfectly kept, the vision of universal rights applying to every individual person has still done much to create greater equality. The logic of the illustrative story grows out of and helps create the worldview in which this expansion of equality makes sense. It is no coincidence that the same new measures preachers who led the way from types to illustrations were also working for the abolition of slavery, the equal rights of women, and a gospel that offered salvation to all on equal terms. A simple narrative of decline would miss the ways that the shift from types to illustrations fit with those reforms in the name of equality for all.

Third, if the story of the shift from type to illustration is told as a narrative of decline, it misses the goodness of the critical consciousness that can recognize a human role in the crafting of types and illustrations. We *do* help make these connections between the things of this age and the things we claim about the age to come. Telling the truth about our role in this process breaks with past generations of Christians in some ways. But in others ways it carries on one of the most important strands that runs through both the Old and the New Testament. It refuses to conflate our work with God's work. It refuses to treat our ideas about God as if they were identical to God. And so this kind of consciousness opens our theological understandings of this world to new kinds of critique. Those openings to critique have had great political significance, but they are not merely useful. They also carry forward the long tradition of refusing to worship idols. Their iconoclasm embodies a severe piety that is needed now every bit as much as it was needed in centuries past. A simple narrative of decline would miss the goodness of this ability to acknowledge the works of our hands for what they are.

The complexities I have tried to sketch here would seem to suggest

---

[10] Alexis de Tocqueville, *Democracy in America*, trans. Harvey Claflin Mansfield and Delba Winthrop (Chicago: University of Chicago Press, 2000), §II.i.iii, 412–14.

a trade-off. We might have gained goods like a stronger ethos of equality and a sharper critical consciousness, but they have cost us the gift of a meaningful world. The price of enlightenment is disenchantment. The terms of this bargain structure many accounts of the rise of modernity.

There is one level at which these stories are true. The shift from type to illustration *does* come with a greater awareness of our role in making meaning. It arises with a loss of confidence in the givenness of the meanings we experience. But to take the loss of the experience of givenness as a sign that there is no givenness is to engage in exactly the idealism that this perspective criticizes in typological thinking. It is to conflate our experience of the world with the world itself. Novelist Saul Bellow named this dynamic precisely. "The educated speak of the disenchanted (a boring) world," he wrote. "But it is not the world, it is my own head that is disenchanted. The world *cannot* be disenchanted."[11]

The world cannot be disenchanted. Because of God's gracious choice, the world was, is, and always will be what John Calvin called the theatre of the glory of God. If we live by this basic trust, then we have reason to believe that God just might find ways to speak through secularized sermon illustrations like the one that Candler used and like the ones we can't help but tell today. For if we trust that the world cannot be disenchanted, then we can trust that stories about this world have meaning not because we tell them in a particular way, but because the world itself—which includes those who tell stories about it—is part of a much larger story, one that we do not write and that gives meaning and direction to history even when we do not recognize it. We can trust that the stones themselves will cry out, not only when we are silent, but in and in spite of the stories that we tell about them.

With that trust in mind, we have new reasons to pay attention to the world. Our trust in the theological significance of this world should lead us to tell stories that cling to the world even more tightly than typology ever did. Our trust that God delights in speaking through the world gives us reason to believe that the diameter of the silkworm's thread matters, and matters theologically. The presence or absence of hammocks matters. It all matters, for the world lives as

---

[11] Saul Bellow, *Humboldt's Gift* (New York: Viking Press, 1975), 203.

the language of God. That we cannot always be certain of our understandings of that language does not change this reality. Nor does our awareness of our role in making the meaning that we attribute to these things. On the contrary, that awareness gives us even more reason to attend to the things of this world, for it is the world itself—not our thoughts about it—that cannot be disenchanted.

The great danger of trusting in the revelatory quality of the world is that we will mistake the way things are for the way things are supposed to be. In assuming the theological significance of the world we can slip into what Theodor Adorno called "magical positivism." This "wide-eyed presentation of mere facts" can only be performed if we suspend the critical consciousness that we have gained at such cost.[12] Even more, it mistakes the ways things end in this age for their final endings, and so gives those who have the power to shape those earthly endings the power to define the meaning of history. It gives death the last word.

Insisting on the theological significance of the empirical world while refusing to let the powers of this age define that significance commits us to proposing different endings for the stories that we tell about the world. One way to do this is to tell stories with "points," just like Candler did. The first significance of these points is *negative*. Proposing a point as the *real* meaning of the story refuses the natural and final qualities of the meanings offered by the powers and principalities of this age. Points of stories, even if we make them, declare our hope for something more. They declare our trust in a story with a better ending. They pledge our resolve to live into the shape of that story.

The declaration of such hope can survive the realization that we have had a hand in making the meanings that we propose. Because we make these points, they are fallible. They remain open to revision. But they are no less hopeful for that. For we fashion these meanings to refuse the closure whereby the way the story ends in this age defines its ultimate meaning. We fashion these meanings to serve as signs that we and all that we perceive are part of a larger story than we can tell. Our consciousness that we have a hand in

---

[12] Theodor Adorno and Walter Benjamin, *The Complete Correspondence, 1928–1940*, ed. Henri Lonitz, transl. Nicholas Walker (Cambridge, MA: Harvard University Press, 2001), 183.

making the meaning that we experience does not rob the world of meaning. The negation of the ending supplied by this age, coupled with a recognition of the made quality of the ending we supply, reveals the world to be yearning for a point to the story that is better than any we could make. When we perceive the world yearning in this way, we find ourselves yearning with it. For we are reminded that we do not know how to pray as we ought. And in this realization we find ourselves groaning with the Holy Spirit, and with all creation, in sighs too deep for words. Those sighs are the most truthful testimony we have to offer. It is the great hymn of the church that waits: Maranantha! Come, Lord Jesus! In and in spite of our intentions, that hymn sings through the stories we preachers use to illustrate our points.

Heard in this way, Bishop Candler's story about the land birds comes to us as good news. Like every preacher, Candler proclaimed a gospel that outran his intentions. His story did more than illustrate a general point about doctrine. It declared that the birds were a sign of something greater than the fact that Columbus and his crew were drawing near to land. The sermon therefore suggested that the real meaning of the story of the landing of those ships was not any of the empirical endpoints that we already know for this story. The real meaning of this event—the point of this story—was not the enrichment of the nations of Europe. It was not the founding of colonies in North America. It was not the death and enslavement of the people who greeted Columbus and his crew and taught them how to make hammocks. Candler's story about the birds insisted that none of these moments was the *real* end of the story.

The real end of the story, as Candler told it, was the arrival of the Reign of God. He described the birds singing in the sails as heralds of this Reign. Thus Candler's story refused the power of anything less than this Reign to define the meaning of that moment in 1492. Even if Candler fashioned the ending himself, it could still break the hold of the powers of this age to define the meaning of this age. And it could reveal this age to be a time of types yearning for fulfillment in their true antitypes, antitypes so lovely that we desire them even when we do not have words to describe them. The fragile, fallible point of the story reveals that moment in 1492 to be groaning for a time when, just as Candler said,

93

The fruits of the Spirit come floating on the bosom of the deep, and the great birds of the kingdom come singing in the sails, and we begin to cry out, "Land ahead!" And, blessed be God, there is land ahead! "Christ in you the hope of glory."

CHAPTER 9

Affirmation and Accountability: Ethical Dimensions of "That Blessed Image"

Ellen Ott Marshall

Centennial Academic Conference Lecture
March 19, 2015

T he subtitle for this lecture takes its language from one of John Wesley's everyday prayers for families. Ted Runyon cites the prayer in his book, *The New Creation*, which greatly informs this lecture. This is the prayer:

> O that we may all receive of [Christ's] fullness, grace upon grace; grace to pardon our sins, and subdue our iniquities; to justify our persons and to sanctify our souls; and to complete that holy change, that renewal of our hearts, whereby we may be transformed into that blessed image wherein thou didst create us.[1]

I am using "that blessed image" in the way Wesley does here—as our beginning and our end; we are created in "that blessed image" and strive to become it. This language affirms the goodness and potential of the human person and the intimate relationship with a loving and gracious God that constitutes the context of our lives.

But I am also using "that blessed image" in the same way we talk about "that blessed assignment" we cannot avoid; "that blessed

---

[1] John Wesley, "Prayers for Families," from *A Collection of Forms of Prayers*, in *The Works of John Wesley*, ed. Thomas Jackson, 3rd ed., 14 vols. (London: Wesleyan Methodist Book Room, 1872; repr. Grand Rapids: Baker Book House, 1979); quoted in Theodore Runyon, *The New Creation: John Wesley's Theology Today* (Nashville: Abingdon Press, 1998), 27.

mandate" we cannot ignore; "that blessed commitment" that complicates our plans. The image of God, when taken seriously, muddies our lives, our politics, and our speech. It does not allow us to divide the world neatly between good guys and bad guys. It binds us to people we might rather get away from. If we take the *imago Dei* seriously, we cannot dismiss anyone as unworthy of care or beyond redemption. "That blessed image" is our greatest affirmation and our most challenging truth.

Searching through the library catalogue using "image of God" as the exact subject yields references to 153 books. When you expand the search to include articles, the yield jumps to 502. If you expand the search even further: all materials that contain the phrase "image of God," over 3,000 items turn up. Of course, to get a real beat on contemporary engagement with the phrase, we need to search in other places, like Google which generates 35,600,000 hits in 0.37 seconds. The "hashtag" *#imageofGod* is quite active on Twitter. There is even an Instagram account and a Tumblr feed for "image of God" —but I needed my 11-year-old daughter to show me those.

The "image of God" does not just enter into contemporary conversation frequently; it enters authoritatively. The doctrine of the *imago Dei* anchors arguments for human rights, economic rights, civil rights, and cultural rights. It grounds ministries serving the homeless, undocumented migrants, and other marginalized persons. It even informs opposing sides in debates over abortion, the death penalty, war, and euthanasia.

By its frequency and weight, the *imago Dei* is massive. And yet, as we know, there is an almost cartoonish discrepancy between this mass of material and the tiny scriptural basis on which it sits. Our colleague and former academic dean, Ian McFarland, makes this point on the opening page of his book, *The Divine Image*. "The key text is, of course, Gen 1:26-27":

> Then God said, 'Let us make humankind in our image, according to our likeness; and let them have dominion over the fish of the sea, and over the birds of the air, and over the cattle, and over all the wild animals of the earth, and over every creeping thing that creeps upon the earth.' So God created humankind in

his image, in the image of God he created them, male and female he created them.[2]

Beyond this key text we find a few more, rather passing references. The geneology offered in Genesis 5 opens with this reminder:
"When God created humankind, he made them in the likeness of
God." In Genesis 9, we find God's covenant with Noah, which includes this mandate: "Whoever sheds the blood of a human, by a human shall that person's blood be shed; for in his own image God
made humankind" (Gen 9:6). We find two more references in the
New Testament. In Paul's first letter to the Corinthians, he mentions
the image of God but adds a distinction based on gender to explain
why women should cover their heads: "For a man ought not to have
his head veiled, since he is the image and reflection of God; but
woman is the reflection of man" (1 Cor 11:7). James also references
the image of God in the course of his appeal to tame the tongue,
which utters both blessings and curses: "With it [the tongue] we
bless the Lord and Father, and with it we curse those who are made
in the likeness of God" (Jas 3:9). McFarland comments, "Though the
phrase is certainly evocative, such a sporadic pattern of use would
seem to suggest caution in according it excessive anthropological
weight." And yet, McFarland continues, theologians since the time
of Irenaeus have viewed the *imago Dei* "as the key to formulating the
Christian doctrine of human being."[3]

Similarly, in my field of Christian ethics, the *imago Dei* features
prominently in moral discernment and ethical argumentation over
social, political, economic, and biomedical questions. Sometimes,
like Paul, Christian ethicists reference the *imago Dei* to make distinctions among persons or to set persons apart from the rest of creation.
In other places, one finds argumentation akin to that of James: concern about the way we treat others in light of the fact that all are
made in the image of God.

What are we to make of the remarkable fertility of these few
verses of Scripture? And should we be concerned about the family
resemblance (or lack thereof) between these verses and their innu-
merable offspring?

---

[2] Ian A. McFarland, *The Divine Image: Envisioning The Invisible God*
(Minneapolis: Fortress Press, 2005), 1.
[3] Ibid.

One way to make sense of the mismatch between the massiveness of the *imago Dei* presently and its scarcity in Scripture is to note the historical nature of a *construing belief.* Writing as psychologist of religion, Juliann Hartt has described a construing belief as a concept through which we interpret the world.[4] For example, I see a yucca plant shooting its white flower up from a burned hillside, and I say, "Ah, resurrection. Life asserts itself even in the midst of death." Now, what is actually happening? Well, although there is apparently dispute over the relationship between yucca plants and fire, there seems to be general agreement that some yucca plants over five years old not only withstand fire, but are actually stimulated to flower because of fire. I am seeing a plant responding to intense heat; but I construe it as resurrection. Construing beliefs also work the other way around. Having lived in southern California, where we were evacuated from our home and watched the hills of our canyon neighborhood burn, only to see those remarkable shoots of white against the deforested hills, I found that resurrection took on additional meaning for me. The sight of the flowering yucca plant standing out against the scorched hillside enriched my understanding of something I had intellectualized but not felt: death does not have the last word; life asserts itself.

Now, I know that my yucca plant and I do not determine the meaning of resurrection. But, as a participant in a dynamic, historical religion I do contribute to it, even if in the smallest of ways. That is, an historical approach to religion perceives and values its development over time through a dynamic process that involves the interaction of texts, communities, and lived experience. Applying the historical sensibility to the image of God, we can see how this central doctrine has accrued meaning over time. The massiveness of the concept currently reflects its historical development as Christians have considered it afresh across time and space rather than sealing it off in a dogmatic fashion.

As a construing belief, the *imago Dei* is informed by our experiences in the world and particularly by our attention to bodies. We understand more fully the profound meaning of the *imago Dei* by

---

[4] Juliann Hartt, "Encounter and Inference in Our Awareness of God," in *The God Experience: Essays in Hope,* ed. Joseph P. Whelan, S.J. (New York: Newman Press, 1971), 49.

truly attending to bodies in their destruction, brokenness, healing, restoration, and transformation. Moreover, we respond to bodies by invoking the *imago Dei*. This theological doctrine carries profound pastoral, political, and rhetorical power with which to speak to the violation of persons, to bear witness to the dignity being denied, and to call for the concern that is warranted. The "image of God in contemporary society," as I understand it then, is not so much an exercise in doctrinal definition as an engagement with an expansive and dynamic project of faith.

Engaging an expansive and dynamic project of faith involves describing the contours that have emerged thus far and at least indicating considerations for further development, if not articulating some parameters for it. I will focus here on historical development during the life of our school. During the twentieth century, we see an emphasis on universality, the insistence upon relationship, and attention to process. These three things—universality, relationality, and process—become essential features of this project of faith called "the image of God in contemporary society."

The Image of God in Contemporary Society

One storyline of the twentieth century is a narrative about violation and assertion of personhood: exploitation of workers and the fights to end child labor and secure a living wage; the denial of political equality and the suffragette movement; the atrocities of the Shoah and the development of the United Nations Declaration on Human Rights; lynching, Jim Crow, segregation and the civil rights movement in the United States; apartheid and black consciousness; political repression, proxy wars, and the preferential option for the poor; homophobic violence and expanded hate crimes legislation; systematic abuse and neglect of people with disabilities and the witness of L'Arche communities.

Clearly, Christians do not stand consistently for affirmation of persons and have often contributed to violation of others. But when Christians resist economic exploitation, political repression, and violation of persons, they regularly invoke the image of God to do so. In these examples, we see the way(s) in which the *imago Dei* undergirds the language of rights. We also see the power of the *imago Dei* to affirm the inherent dignity of each and every person, within structures that systematically deny personhood.

For example, in response to the exploitation of workers and the use of child labor, the Federal Council of Churches drafted the 1908 Social Creed that called on all churches to stand "for equal rights and complete justice for all men in all stations of life,"for safe working conditions and a living wage, for the abolition of child labor, and the abatement of poverty.[5] One hundred years later, the National Council of Churches issued its "Social Creed for the Twenty-First Century," a document which must, by necessity, continue to appeal for safe working conditions, a living wage, and an end to child labor, poverty, and hunger. Unlike its predecessor, though, this document makes explicit the theological affirmations that undergird the language of rights: "the full humanity of each woman, man, and child, all created in the divine image as individuals of infinite worth."[6] These documents constitute but a few pages of the historical record that reflects Christian attempts to illuminate the gross inconsistency between human beings as created in the image of God and human beings as exploited in the economic machinery of society. In the rich tradition of Roman Catholic social thought, the dignity of the human person mandates economic, social, and political rights and also constitutes the criterion by which one judges policies and practices. Building on papal statements since *Rerum Novarum* in 1891, the US Catholic Bishops issued *Economic Justice for All* in 1986, which includes as a central theme the assertion that: "Every economic decision and institution must be judged in light of whether it protects or undermines the dignity of the human person."[7]

As this historical record demonstrates, "the image of God in contemporary society"serves as a Christian criterion for justice. Do the policies and practices of institutional life protect or undermine human dignity? Do they reflect or deny the image of God that gives all

---

[5] Federal Council of Churches, "The Social Creed of the Churches," (1908), http://nationalcouncilofchurches.us/common-witness/1908/social-creed.php.

[6] National Council of Churches, "Social Creed for the Twenty-First Century," http://www.ncccusa.org/news/ga2007.socialcreed.html.

[7] National Conference of Catholic Bishops, *Economic Justice for All: Pastoral Letter on Catholic Social Teaching and the U.S. Economy* (Washington, DC: National Conference of Catholic Bishops, 1986), ix.

persons infinite worth? But the image of God is also more than a criterion for justice; it is a theological statement. Economic structures that assign people instrumental value rather than inherent value are not only unjust; they are sacrilegious. Economic policies that treat the poor as waste rather than recognizing infinite worth are not only unfair; they are a desecration of the holy.

Archbishop Desmond Tutu makes this same point when he denounces the violence of political repression. After asserting that human beings are endowed with dignity and worth, he continues:

> To treat such persons as if they were less than this, to oppress them, to trample their dignity underfoot, is not just evil as it surely must be; it is not just painful as it frequently must be for the victims of injustice and oppression. It is positively blasphemous, for it is tantamount to spitting in the face of God.[8]

Consider afresh the power of this language, particularly in contexts of systematic oppression and violence, contexts where persons are attacked, marginalized, and silenced because of an attribute that renders them "less than." In these places, which of course are all around us, this universal theological affirmation of personhood is, in Tutu's words, both "marvelously exhilarating"and "staggering." "We are all, each one of us, created in the image of God."[9]

Think about the contexts of gross inequality that you know and the power of affirming inherent worth and dignity there. It is empowering, inspiring, affirming, good, true, and right to walk the streets where yet another African American person has been shot by a police officer and bear witness to the power of the *imago Dei* by declaring: Black Lives Matter. It is empowering, inspiring, affirming, good, true, and right to stand outside of a private detention center in south Georgia and insist that the people who have no papers and no status are in fact bearers of the divine image. It is empowering, inspiring, affirming, good, true, and right to embrace those kicked to the curb because of addiction, poverty, untreated mental illness, or screw ups of various kinds and say to them: you are God's beloved in whom God is well pleased. It is empowering, inspiring, affirming,

---

[8] Desmond M. Tutu, foreword to *Christianity and Human Rights: An Introduction*, ed. John Witte Jr. and Frank S. Alexander (Cambridge: Cambridge University Press, 2011), 3.

[9] Ibid., 2.

good, true, and right to insist that violence against any body—gay, straight, cis, or transgendered—is a desecration of the holy.

Archbishop Tutu describes the universal affirmation of personhood as marvelously exhilarating and also staggering, and I appreciate that word. We must, surely, stumble a bit when we recall that all persons are created in God's image—not only the oppressed, but also the oppressor; not only the victim, but also the perpetrator; not only the advocate for justice, but also the guardian and beneficiary of the status quo. The officer who shoots the unarmed man; the anti-immigrant protestor who blocks the bus of unaccompanied minors and screams at them; the mother who planned the death of her husband and lied about it; the abuser, the terrorist. Each and every one of them is also created in the image of God.

It is even more arresting to realize—to feel—that the perpetrators of violence are not only made in the image of God like I am; but that they are made in the image of God with me. Our relationship to the Creator locks us into relationship with one another. The *imago Dei* is not only a declaration of personhood; it is a declaration of relationship. In the language of Walter Rauschenbusch, "our roots run down into the eternal life of God."[10] We share a common root system. In this way, "the image of God in contemporary society" not only grounds universal human rights; but it also establishes the context for our relationships and responsibilities to one another. And, with this argument, the *imago Dei* emerges as a theological foundation for restorative justice and processes of reconciliation.

This is the point at which my argument takes a decidedly, though not uniquely, Wesleyan turn. In *The New Creation*, Candler's beloved emeritus professor Ted Runyon describes the theology beneath Methodist social witness in the areas of human rights, the environment, and poverty. He highlights a soteriology that "sees the 'great salvation' . . . as nothing less than a new creation transforming all dimensions of human existence, both personal and social."[11] Central to this is a particular understanding of the image of God, which reinforces relationality. Professor Runyon explains that Wesley understood "the image more relationally, not so much as something

---

[10] Walter Rauschenbusch, *A Theology for the Social Gospel* (New York: Macmillan, 1917; Nashville: Abingdon Press, 1990), 186.

[11] Runyon, *The New Creation*, 5.

humans possess as the way they relate to God and live out that relation in the world."[12] Wesley described three ways that human beings bear the image of God. The "natural image" refers to the endowments that make us "capable of God," or able to enter into relationship with God. These include understanding, will, and freedom. Recognizing that the natural image echoes the more traditional views on capacities, Runyon argues that even here we see that the qualities of the natural image are in the service of relationship. Wesley also described the political image to capture the place of human beings in governing the earth. Human beings are assigned a place of privilege and responsibility, but, again, this place is nested in a context of relationship to the creator of all things. Runyon explains: "Humanity is the image of God insofar as the benevolence of God is reflected in human action toward the rest of creation."[13] In the moral image of God, the human being receives continually from the creator and mediates to the world that which is received.[14] This is the context of Wesley's proposal for "spiritual respiration"—the ongoing breathing in of the spirit of God and channeling that spirit out into the world. This "unceasing presence of God" underscores our relationship with the creator; a relationship that we maintain through "a life of service to God, our fellow human beings, and all creation."[15]

We find here reinforcement of some thoughts about the image of God that we have already heard: that it is universal and relational. But we also gain something, namely attention to the processes by which the image of God is restored or diminished in humanity. One of many things I have learned through studying violence is that an act of violence is never an isolated and encapsulated event; it is always part of a larger story. Indeed, I find it much more accurate to think about narratives of violence rather than "an act of violence." Similarly, the violation or denial of the image of God is not an isolated and encapsulated event; rather violation and denial are always part of a larger story. The image of God may be violated in a moment, but it is diminished over time through repetition of

---

[12] Ibid., 13.
[13] Ibid., 17.
[14] Ibid., 18.
[15] Ibid.

abuse, systematic discrimination, or a never-ending barrage of humiliation and ridicule.

We see this again and again when we take time to learn the history of someone who has committed a crime. This is where my argument takes a decidedly, though not exclusively, literary turn, as I search for language that captures the experiences I am trying to describe. "A Jury of Her Peers" is a short story written by Susan Glaspell and based on her 1916 play, "Trifles." The story opens on a farmhouse where a man has been killed. The man's wife has been arrested under suspicion of murder. The county attorney, the sheriff, and the neighbor who discovered the body explore the farmhouse looking for evidence and signs of motive. Meanwhile, the sheriff's wife and the neighbor's wife deal in trifles, gathering belongings to take to the woman in jail and sharing impressions of her life. Fingering pieces of a quilt, the neighbor, Mrs. Hale, recalls the yellow dress that Mrs. Wright wore when she "sang so pretty in the choir."[16] She then unveils a picture of a woman transformed, from youthful and vibrant, to isolated and silent. Of the dead man, John Wright, she says: "just to pass the time of day with him was like a cold wind getting to the bones."[17] Mrs. Hale then rebukes herself for not coming to visit Mrs. Wright, not checking up on her, not reaching out to her. "That's a crime," she says, "who's going to punish that?"[18]

As we explore the details of a life, we see the distinctions between perpetrator and victim blur and shift. We see the formation and transformation of personhood over time. We see the ways in which the *imago Dei* gets buried beneath acts of abuse, patterns of neglect, and speech that belittles and betrays. And, most powerfully I think, we see that this burial occurs in the life of those inflicting violence as well as those receiving it.

For example, the recent literature on moral injury describes the impact of violence on soldiers. Rita Nakashima Brock and Gabreilla Lettini explain: "Moral injury results when soldiers violate their core moral beliefs, and in evaluating their behavior negatively, they feel they no longer live in a reliable, meaningful world and can no

---

[16] Susan Glaspell, *A Jury of Her Peers* (Mankato, MN: Creative Education, 1993), 25.
[17] Ibid., 36.
[18] Ibid., 43.

longer be regarded as decent human beings."[19] Placing Wesley's three dimensions of the image of God in conversation with the descriptions of moral injury is illuminating. When one violates one's conscience—whether in the performance of duty or in the madness of war—the natural image of God is diminished. Violation of conscience constitutes an attack on understanding, freedom, and will—the very qualities that give us the capacity to connect with God, according to Wesley. In the description from Brock and Lettini, we can hear the diminishment of the political image—by which we represent a benevolent God in the world—and the moral image—by which we receive and channel the grace of God in the world.

Moral injury can lead veterans to feelings of worthlessness, remorse, and despair; they may feel as if they lost their souls in combat and are no longer who they were. Connecting emotionally to others becomes impossible for those trapped inside the walls of such feelings. In a chapter titled, "War Changes You," Brock and Lettini include an extract from a poem by Camillo Mac Bica, a former U.S. Marine Corps officer and veteran of the Vietnam War. The poem, "Warrior's Dance (Tai Chi Chuan)," gives expression to this transformation.

> I fear I am no longer alien to this horror.
> I am, I am, I am the horror.
> I have lost my humanity
> And have embraced the insanity of war.
> The monster and I are one.
> . . . .
> The blood of innocents forever stains my soul!
> The transformation is complete
> And I can never return.
> *Mea culpa, mea culpa, mea maxima culpa.*[20]

As Brock and Lettini note, Bica insists that "no one truly 'recovers' from war. No one is ever made whole again." So he strives every day

[19] Rita Nakashima Brock and Gabriella Lettini, eds., *Soul Repair: Recovering from Moral Injury after War* (Boston: Beacon Press, 2013), xv.

[20] Camillo Mac Bica, "Warrior's Dance (Tai Chi Chuan)," in *Worthy of Gratitude: Why Veterans May Not Want to be Thanked for Their Service in War* (New York: Gnosis Press, 2016), pp. 26–27. Used by permission. Cited in Brock and Lettini, 20.

"to forgive and absolve [him]self of guilt and to live with the wounds of war that will never heal."[21]

If violation of the image of God is not an act, but a process, the same things must be said of restoration or recovery of the image of God. This too is a process, a narrative of healing, or restoration. It is the journey of grace, the process of becoming that which we were created to be. The *imago Dei* is our beginning and our end. What is so crucial, though, is that this journey is not a solo trek. The image of God is restored in us as we receive and reflect it in the world. This process is a social process; it involves an interactional dynamic. Another veteran profiled in Brock and Lettini's work gives expression to this. Camilo Ernesto Mejia is a veteran of the Iraq War who describes his pre-enlistement life as "self-absorbed." He did not see the connections between his problems and the problems of others. But his "experience in Iraq changed that," he says.

> Moral injury is painful, yet it has also returned a sense of humanity that had been missing from my life for longer than I can remember. I have come to believe that the transformative power of moral injury cannot be found in the pursuit of our own moral balance as an end goal, but in the journey of repairing the damage we have done unto others.[22]

Repairing the damage we have done to others often begins with affirmation.

All persons are created in the image of God, with inherent worth, value, and dignity. Recognizing the relational nature of the image of God, the process of transformation continues through practices of accountability. We remain accountable to one another for our transgressions and for our mutual healing. The image of God is not only a theological affirmation; it is also an ethical imperative. "That blessed image" affirms us and calls us to task.

In reality, our task is utter nonsense. We are called to affirm the image of God in a world where the human body is often treated like garbage. I think of mangled bodies dumped like refuse, desperate bodies sorting through trash bins, beaten and raped bodies as the receptacles of hatred, neglected bodies considered to be a waste of time, depleted

---

[21] Brock and Lettini, 75.
[22] Ibid., 89.

bodies used up and discarded, bodies strapped with explosives and detonated. How do we affirm the image of God in these bodies, let alone the bodies of the ones who trash them? My mind goes, thankfully if sadly, to a poem by Mary Oliver:

> I want to sing a song
> for a body I saw
> crumpled
> and without a name
>
> but clearly someone young
> who had not yet lived his life
> and never would.
> How shall I do this?
>
> What kind of song
> would serve such a purpose?
> This poem may never end,
> for what answer does it have
>
> for anyone
> in this distant,
> comfortable country,
> simply looking on?
>
> Clearly
> he had a weapon in his hands.
> I think
> he could have been no more than twenty.
>
> I think, whoever he was,
> of whatever country,
> he might have been my brother,
> were the world different.
>
> I think
> he would not have been lying there
> were the world different.
> I think
>
> if I had known him,
> on his birthday,
> I would have made for him
> a great celebration.[23]

Mary Oliver titles this poem, "Iraq." But we could title it Syria,

[23] Mary Oliver, "Iraq," in *Red Bird: Poems by Mary Oliver* (Boston: Beacon Press, 2008), 48–49. Used by permission.

Palestine, Israel, South Sudan, Nigeria, Ukraine, Ferguson, Staten Island, Los Angeles, or Jackson, GA. It is the sentiment that moves me; the declaration, the resolve: I would have made for him a great celebration. The stark contrast between the crumpled, nameless body and the honoree at a birthday party captures the jarring difference between the degradation of bodies all around us and the promise of the *imago Dei*.

One afternoon in the spring of 2015, I sat in my office with a student who was very involved in the advocacy and witness for Kelly Gissendaner. Kelly Gissendaner was a graduate of the theology certificate program in the women's prison where many Candler faculty and students have worked over the last fifteen years. Kelly was a pen pal of Jürgen Moltmann's and a pastoral presence to other women incarcerated at Lee Arrendale prison north of Atlanta. And, she was on death row. Her execution was postponed by a storm in February 2015; and she was granted a stay of execution due to "cloudy drugs" one month later. The advocacy, appeals, and pastoral support for Kelly and the incarcerated women who knew her continued throughout the summer. However, the State of Georgia went through with the execution of Kelly Gissendaner on September 15, 2015.

On that spring day in my office, this student broke down in tears. She felt overwhelmed by the sadness of the situation and exhausted by the time and energy required for advocacy. But her tears turned to sobs when she shared a fact she learned from others during the long evening vigil in Jackson, Georgia, where the executions take place. There had already been two people executed in Georgia that year: Andrew Brannon, a Vietnam veteran with diagnosed PTSD, was executed for killing a sheriff's deputy in 1998; and Warren Hill, a man with documented intellectual disability, was executed for killing his girlfriend in 1985 and a fellow inmate in 1990. Fewer than twelve people showed up to stand vigil for them. Fewer than twelve people were there to affirm the dignity of a man; fewer than twelve people were there to channel God's loving presence into that cruel and dehumanizing place.

Surely, affirming the *imago Dei*—that each and every person is created in God's image—is one of the great prophetic challenges for the twenty-first century. But the way that the Candler community responded to the physical and structural violence in Ferguson (and beyond) and to the scheduled execution of Kelly Gissendaner continues to give me tremendous hope. In their actions and their speech, Candler students not only affirm the image of God that narratives of violence have diminished and disregarded; but they also bear that image into this world of great need and pain. During the vigil for Kelly that was held in Cannon Chapel, our colleague Liz Bounds read two poems that Kelly wrote in a creative writing class while pursuing her theology certificate. I invite you to listen to a few stanzas of her poem called "Change Has Come" as a description of transformation and restoration of the image of God.

> Can a person really change?
> Can a person really be different tomorrow?
> Opened up to love
> Learning to walk by faith
> Not offset by fear
> Living not in yesterday
>
> To embrace [this] love
> And let go of the hatred of yesterday
> To find your faith
> And to walk in your change
> For a better tomorrow
> A future without fear[24]

Conclusion

In this conclusion, I need to re-orient myself in relationship to the subject, to set down (temporarily) the task of proclamation and pick up the task of description and reflection. I have described the image of God not in terms of doctrinal definition, but as a dynamic and historical project of faith. Of course, the danger in dynamic, historical projects is that we find ourselves with a hodge-podge of loosely related images and experiences construed in light of loosely interpreted biblical metaphors that make loose reference to an ad hoc collection of scripture. In short, we wind up with one of my kitchen drawers—a collection of things that are sort of related to one another but belong in more carefully organized and labeled drawers

---

[24] Kelly Gissendaner, "Change Has Come," unpublished manuscript from creative writing course, Elizabeth Bounds, instructor (Georgia: Lee Arrendale Prison, 2016). Used by permission.

in someone else's kitchen. To my mind, understanding the *imago Dei* apart from its accrual of meaning over time is neither possible nor appealing. I take the massive presence of this concept to reflect its pastoral power to uplift those who are downtrodden, its political power to affirm those who have been repressed, and its annoying relational power that binds us up with others no matter what. I celebrate that. But I also recognize that the dynamic, historical nature of the image of God constitutes another challenge for the twenty-first century.

How do we continue to live with the concept of the *imago Dei* in a dynamic way that gives meaning to our lives and vibrancy to the concept and yet avoid the pitfalls of fragmentation, incoherence, instrumentalism, and idolatry? We all, in our daily lives, must face the challenge of affirming and reflecting the image of God in the world. But, this challenge of maintaining dynamism, vibrancy, and coherence, while avoiding fragmentation, instrumentalism, and idolatry — this is the particular challenge that sits at the feet of theological education, particularly theological education that seeks to be prophetic.

And, so, it would not hurt to commit Wesley's prayer to memory. Here it is again:

O that we may all receive of [Christ's] fullness, grace upon grace; grace to pardon our sins, and subdue our iniquities; to justify our persons and to sanctify our souls; and to complete that holy change, that renewal of our hearts, whereby we may be transformed into that blessed image wherein thou didst create us.[25]

---

[25] Quoted in Runyon, *The New Creation*, 27.

CHAPTER 10

To Whom Can We Go?

Thomas G. Long

Centennial Academic Conference Sermon
March 19, 2014
Text: John 6:60-69

A great deal of the sixth chapter of the Gospel of John is given over to the recounting of a rather long dialogical sermon that Jesus preaches in the synagogue at Capernaum. This is the sermon where Jesus says, "I am the bread of life . . . come down from heaven."

Here is how John describes the disciples' response to Jesus' synagogue sermon:

> When many of his disciples heard it, they said, "This teaching is difficult; who can accept it?" But Jesus, being aware that his disciples were complaining about it, said to them, "Does this offend you? Then what if you were to see the Son of Man ascending to where he was before? It is the spirit that gives life; the flesh is useless. The words that I have spoken to you are spirit and life. But among you there are some who do not believe." For Jesus knew from the first who were the ones that did not believe, and who was the one that would betray him. And he said, "For this reason I have told you that no one can come to me unless it is granted by the Father." Because of this many of his disciples turned back and no longer went about with him. So Jesus asked the twelve, "Do you also wish to go away?" Simon Peter answered him, "Lord, to whom can we go? You have the words of eternal life. We have come to believe and know that you are the Holy One of God."

One Sunday morning some years ago, in a church in Charlotte, North Carolina, the worshipers had made their way about a third of the way through the eleven o'clock service. They had sung the opening hymn and the scripture lessons had been read. The preacher had adjusted the pulpit microphone and was just about to begin the sermon, when suddenly a man, a stranger, stood up in the balcony and announced in a loud and clear voice, "I have a word from the Lord." Heads swiveled around in surprise; people craned their necks to see who this intruder might be. But they never learned who he was and they never heard whatever word from God this man had on his heart, because almost instantly a gaggle of alarmed ushers bounded like gazelles up into the balcony and muscled the man gently but firmly down the stairs, out the doors, and into the street.

Ironic isn't it? Every Sunday, preachers like me stand in pulpits like this and look out onto congregations like you and say, "I have a word from the Lord," and nobody flinches. There is no wary apprehension; no ushers come bounding into the chancel to muscle us into the streets. Now I am not complaining, this is a good thing. But according to the Book of Hebrews, "the Word of God is living and active, sharper than any two-edged sword" (Heb 4:12). It seems to me that an announcement that this Word is about to be proclaimed ought to at least increase alertness, if not tension.

Maybe it takes an unexpected voice, from an unexpected angle, to refresh our memories about the perils and power of the proclaimed Word of God.

Now look, I suspect that the guy in the balcony was probably a crank, a couple of quarts low on reality, but we don't know that for sure. We also have stories of the authentic Word of God coming from unexpected people and places. He might have been a Jeremiah, another intruder who had a word of God burning like fire in his bones. He might have been an Amos, who also crashed a worship service without invitation and said to an astonished clergyman named Amaziah, "I am no prophet, nor a prophet's son— I've never been to seminary, and I'm not ordained—but I've got a Word from the Lord: 'Woe to you who are at ease in Zion'" (cf. Amos 7:14, 6:1).

Or he might have been like Jesus in the synagogue at Capernaum that day who spoke from an unexpected angle with an unexpected voice and disturbed the worship service. I wonder if the leadership at Capernaum wished that they had a couple of burly ushers to muscle him into the street, because according to the Gospel of John, by the time Jesus had said what he wanted to say that day, the whole congregation was in an uproar. Many of his followers had washed their hands of him and turned away, and even his closest disciples were shaking their heads in dismay and saying, "This teaching is difficult; who can accept it?" (John 6:60). This is a hard word.

Well, there are a lot of hard words in the Christian faith, and maybe it would be good for us to hear again the hard word that Jesus proclaimed that day—even on this occasion when we are celebrating Candler's centennial. Because I think John wants us to know that Jesus continues to preach that sermon, and not just in Capernaum, but here as well. Maybe Jesus preaches today from the balcony, in an unexpected place and from an unexpected angle. Perhaps even on this day of festivity, it would be good for us to understand what it is that is so unsettling about what Jesus said. It might give some texture and depth to our celebration.

The disciples said the Jesus' sermon was a hard word, hard to receive. There are a lot of hard words in the Christian faith and the gospel. "You shall love the Lord your God with all your heart, and with all your soul, and with all your strength, and with all your mind; and your neighbor as yourself" (Luke 10:27). That's hard. "If anyone strikes you on the right cheek, turn the other also" (Matt 5:39). That's hard. "If anyone wants to sue you and take your coat, give your cloak as well" (Matt 5:40). That's hard. "I say to you, Love your enemies and pray for those who persecute you" (Matt 5:44). That's hard. Or how about this one? "Start a theological school at the eve of World War I and walk with it step-by-step through a hundred years, nourishing it as you go in faith, until you arrive at the point you can say at its centennial, 'It has a strong mission and an excellent faculty, and wonderful students and loyal alumni, and a passionate commitment to the gospel and social justice.'" That's hard.

Maybe what upset the disciples in the synagogue that day was that Jesus had given them one more hard word on top of others. Jesus was piling on, giving them yet another demanding word in a long list of demands that God had already placed on them. They said, "This teaching is difficult. Who can accept it?" But the fascinating thing is that Jesus will not accept that complaint: "You say this teaching is difficult, but I think you mean *offensive*," said Jesus. "Are you *offended*?" (cf. John 6:60-61).

The Greek translated here as *offended* is better translated as *scandalized*. "You say hard," Jesus responded, "but I really think you are scandalized." There's a difference, you know. Hard is demanding.

Scandal is an affront to something we hold dear and cherish. Hard is difficult to do; scandal is hard to stomach. Hard makes you want to say, "O Lord, where will I get the strength." But scandal wants you to say "O Lord, I'm out of here." Jesus knew that, and that's why he said, "Everyone else has gone away, do you also want to go away?"

What is it that Jesus said that day that was so scandalous? You look over the words and nothing jumps out particularly. He said to labor not for the food that does not last, but to labor for the food that endures into eternity. He said that he was the bread of life come down from heaven and that those who come to him will never be hungry. He said that those who believe in him will never thirst and that he was the one come from heaven to do the will of the one who sent him. Those are beautiful words, lovely metaphors, the kind of things we say at funerals to give people comfort, not offense or scandal. But of course it was not the metaphors that were scandalous; it was the metaphor maker who was scandalous. It was not the metaphors that were scandalous, it was Jesus who was scandalous, the Jesus who said, "Today these metaphors have become flesh, and I dwell among you." It was not the religious poetry that they had that offended them; it was the fact that he wouldn't leave it at the level of religious poetry. The poetry began to sing in him, took on life in him, and he was the one who stood there, no ordinary synagogue preacher but the voice of the one who comes from the burning bush, "I AM who I AM." "I *am* the bread of life, I *am* the food that endures into eternity." It is one thing to talk about the bread of life as manna, it's another thing to have the bread of life standing there in the flesh, looking you in the eye and asking you to make a choice.

You know second-order discourse is always safer and more comfortable than first-order discourse. And in the life of the church and in the life of the theological academy, it is very appropriate that we engage a lot of the time in second-order discourse. We talk *about* the Bible, and we talk *about* the Christian faith, and we talk *about* the church and God and Christ and the Spirit. What makes us nervous is when second-order discourse suddenly becomes first-order discourse. It is one thing to exegete the phrase "The bread of heaven." It is another thing to encounter the bread of heaven in the flesh, to look it in the eye: "I am the bread of heaven. Choose you this day whom you will serve."

Peggy Payne beautifully gets at this "scandal" of first-order discourse in her witty novel *Revelation*. The novel is about the Reverend Swain Hammond. He is a Presbyterian minister, well- educated, serving a progressive-leaning church in Chapel Hill, North Carolina. It is a congregation of university professors and professionals, or as Swain puts it himself, "Bright and interesting people." He is in his backyard one afternoon, lighting the barbecue and drinking a beer, when suddenly God speaks to him, audibly. It sounds like an amplified voice speaking in the distance, but it's unmistakably the divine voice. The voice says, "Know that truth is." Just that. "Know that truth is." Ambiguous, but what is not ambiguous is that Swain knows in his soul he has been directly addressed by the living God, and it panics him, or better, it scandalizes him. He wonders what he will say to his polite, well-educated congregation. He imagines himself in the pulpit looking out at them, telling them about this experience and horror creeping over their faces as they contemplate the possibility that their minister believes he has been spoken to by God. He says to himself, "They are going to ask me to move on, I'm going to have to serve one of those churches with buses."[1]

Diane Komp is a professor emeritus of pediatric oncology at the Yale School of Medicine. She says that when she was a young physician she would have described herself as a post-Christian agnostic. But a number of experiences with her patients, dramatic experiences, experiences she calls "windows on heaven," opened up for her a possibility of a renewal of faith. Her patients were all dying children, and one of them was a lovely seven-year-old girl named Anna, who was suffering from leukemia. Dr. Komp, the little girl's parents, and the hospital chaplain were at her bedside when she died. Dr. Komp reported that just seconds before Anna died, one of those things happened that was an intrusion of the holy into the mundane. Anna mustered just enough strength to sit up in bed and she said, "The angels, Mommy, do you see them? They're so beautiful! Do you hear them singing? I have never heard such beautiful singing!" And then she was gone. Dr. Komp said the parents received this as the most precious blessing that they could have possibly ever received. But the hospital chaplain, more comfortable with the second-

---

[1] Peggy Payne, *Revelation: A Novel* (New York: Simon & Schuster, 1988), 38–45.

order discourse of psychotherapy, fled from the room in panic, scandalized by what had happened, leaving the agnostic physician and the grief-stricken parents to deal with this mystery that transcends all understanding.[2]

Part of the scandal of Jesus is not just what he said but who he was. What he said was first-order discourse because he himself was the Word in the flesh. Everything he said, he embodied, calling on his hearers, and on us, not just to reflect on his words but to make life-changing decisions and choices.

But there is one more scandal in this text, the most scandalous thing really, and it was taught to me not by a biblical scholar, but by, of all people, Mitt Romney.

When Jesus said, "I am the bread of life come down from heaven, if you do not chew on my body and drink my blood you have no life in you." his words were a flat contradiction of the Torah. For example, in Leviticus God says, "If any man of Israel drinks blood I will turn my face away, you shall not drink blood" (Lev 17:10). This is not because blood is disgusting or a contaminant, quite to the contrary it is because blood is life. Blood is the life of the animal and people have no right to take that life. Because God is the God of life and God gives the gift of life, human beings shall not take life. That's the deepest scandal of what Jesus is saying here. He is saying to us, "I want you to take my life. I want you eat my flesh and to drink my blood, to take my life into you. Indeed, if you do not take my life into you, you do not have life at all."

That's where Mitt Romney comes in. In the 2012 presidential campaign, Romney knew that his wealth was a political liability. He hardly went a day that some reporter did not ask him about the number of houses that he had or the number of Cadillacs his wife drove or how he planned to relate to the 47 percent. He and his advisers knew that he could not deny his wealth. That would have been ridiculous. So he had to figure out some way to respond to these questions, and his advisers came up with one. Whenever anybody asked him about his wealth, he would bow his head demurely and modestly and then look up and say, "I've done well," and then he would proceed to say how doing well prepared him for

---

[2] Diane Komp, *A Window to Heaven: When Children See Life in Death* (Grand Rapids: Zondervan, 1992), 28–29.

leadership, wise governance, and so on. By doing this, Romney could congratulate himself for achieving wealth, but without seeming boastful, and then turn his "doing well" into a political asset.

Romney's response—that modestly spoken "I've done well"—irritated the heck out of me, and I finally realized that what irritated the heck out of me was the chill of recognition. This wasn't just what Romney said. It's what I say. That's what I do. It's what most of us say and do. Someone praises us: "Your children are wonderful, they're so smart and poised and able, you all are marvelous parents." We pause, lower our head, and reply: "We've been lucky, we've done well." Someone says: "Your church is fantastic, your ministry is one of terrific leadership. Look at all the young families that are involved in your church. You're bucking the trend here, there's such a positive energy and optimism, you're a fantastic minister." (Pause, lower your head): "I'm blessed, I've done well." Or: "Oh, professor think about your career, the books that you've published, the articles, the impact you've made on your field, what a fantastic teacher you are." (Pause, bow): "I've done well." "Candler—one hundred years, oh look at the new buildings, the sparkling new online DMin program, you are a leader in theological education." (Pause, bowed head): "We've done well."

And what Jesus in the synagogue at Capernaum does is to expose the deep anxiety in all of us, a fear that when we get to the end of life that's the only blessing we will have, that the only blessing we can possibly have is self-congratulation. Underneath this is the truth that we deeply yearn for another kind of blessing, for the blessing that comes not from ourselves but from God, the blessing that was uttered at the beginning of life and that we pray will be said over us at the end—the voice of God saying, "This is my daughter in whom I delight, this is my son in whom I am well pleased." Jesus stands in the synagogue and says, "You do not have the resources to get yourself that blessing. That blessing comes only to those who feast upon me. Without this bread, without this drink, you have no life. So are you going to stay or are you going to go?"

To which Peter speaks for us all, "Lord, to whom can we go? You have the words of eternal life."

This is Candler's centennial. I don't imagine that any of us will be here for the bicentennial, but I wonder what it will be like. I wonder if Candler will be bricks and mortar still, or whether it will be floating on the ether of some technology we haven't yet even dreamed of. I wonder if it will still be United Methodist or whether Christians a century from now will have left denominations far behind. I don't know what Candler's bicentennial will be like. But I do know that if there is a bicentennial it will be because Candler has continued to ask, as it has over the last century, "O Lord, give us the words of life. If you do not give us life, if we do not feast upon you, we have no life in us. To whom else could we go? You have the words of life."

Amen.

CHAPTER 11

Understanding and Hope in a Time of Climate Change: A Conversation with the Bible

Carol A. Newsom

Centennial Academic Conference Lecture
March 19, 2015

If the faculty of the Candler School of Theology had gathered in March of 1915 to think about the coming century and the challenges it would present, the topic of "the care of the earth" would not have been on the agenda. The relationship between humankind and the earth not only felt different to them. It was different than it is today. That is not to say that they would have been unaware of the transformations that were taking place through new technologies. Steamships and railroads made it possible for many, many people to travel far greater distances than previously. The newest technologies of motion—the automobile and the airplane—were just beginning to make their impact. By 1915 the telephone was magically bringing distant people together. And the radio and motion pictures were just beginning to make their potential felt. There were reasons to be anxious. The Great War was showing the destructive power of industrial technology, but even this event was generally enfolded within an optimistic narrative of human progress. And the world itself still felt enormous. The romance of the Victorian age explorers who journeyed through tropical Africa and Asia and South America was still recent, and Peary and Amundsen had led the first expeditions to reach the North and South poles less than six years before the founding of Candler. Quite literally, no one in 1915 envisioned that human actions could put in jeopardy the very systems that sustain life on the planet.

THE VOCATION OF THEOLOGY

Now, in the twenty-first century, it is all too evident that we not only can but have put them in jeopardy. As we look toward the next century, we have to contemplate the near certainty that our collective actions are rapidly altering the very climate of the earth in ways that will require thousands, if not tens of thousands, of years to repair. And some of the changes—notably, the extinction of species—will be permanent. In recent years scientists have seriously been considering whether humankind's impact on the planet and its systems has been so profound that the current geological age should not be called the Holocene (the "recent" epoch) but the Anthropocene (the "human" epoch). Our somewhat belated grasp of this situation requires urgent response on many levels—practical, political, economic—but also, and not least, theological.

I have been surprised that, even among many people who consider themselves to have a theology of care for the earth, there is so little understanding of the severity and immediacy of the climate crisis. We have treated it as if it were simply a chronic problem, like poverty or violence. But it is an acute problem demanding immediate action—or else. Though it is not my intention here merely to be depressing, it is important to begin by making clear the situation in which we find ourselves. It is a frightening story, but I do not see it as a story of doom. Before we can put things into an interpretive framework, however, we need delineate the situation itself.

Three recently published reports give us a clear sense of the situation that we face and the urgency of the response required. One is from the Intergovernmental Panel on Climate Change and addresses the basic physical science of climate change.[1] The second is from the World Bank concerning the effects of climate change on agriculture and the struggle to end poverty in the developing world.[2] The third is from the Pentagon on the relation between climate

---

[1] IPCC, 2014: Summary for policymakers. In: *Climate Change 2014: Impacts, Adaptation, and Vulnerability. Part A: Global and Sectoral Aspects. Contribution of Working Group II to the Fifth Assessment Report of the Intergovernmental Panel on Climate Change* (Cambridge: Cambridge University Press, 2014), 1–32. Available online at http://www.ipcc.ch/report/ar5/wg1/.

[2] *Turn Dowm the Heat: Why a 4°C Warmer World Must Be Avoided. A Report for the World Bank by the Potsdam Institute for Climate Impact Research and Climate Analytics* (Washington, DC: The World Bank, 2012). Available

change and geopolitical conflict.[3] Let me lift up a few of their conclusions.

First, climate change is not something that may happen in the future. It is happening now. We see its footprint in extreme weather events. Although scientists are rightly cautious about tracing the causes of any specific event to global warming, what is scientifically clear is that the already reached increase of 0.8 degrees Celsius above pre-industrial levels has resulted in the increased frequency and intensity of extreme weather events: floods, heat waves, and prolonged drought. But the devastation to our environment is not just from extreme events. What seem to us to be relatively small changes also have dramatic effects. In the western part of the country, dead forests are appearing from Mexico to Alaska. Winter temperatures are no longer cold enough to kill off the pine beetles that destroy the trees. The destruction will not end until these forests are functionally extinct. The enormous quantity of dead biomass leads to fears of catastrophic wildfires, which burn in ways that sometimes prevent the pattern of recovery one could previously assume. Moreover, an increase in temperatures to 1.5 degrees Celsius (nearly twice what we have experienced to this point) is actually already locked into our future. And that is if we do everything right from here on out.

What does the future of our climate hold? We have the scientific knowledge to know what we need to do. The economic impacts of addressing climate change would certainly be far less than those that will result from ignoring it. But we seem to lack the political wisdom and will to address the problem. There are, to be sure, some hopeful signs. But even as environmental scientists cheer these accomplishments, they also rightly point out that, even if all current commitments are honored, they will not be sufficient to keep global warming below the threshhold of 2 degrees Celsius that has been considered the critical benchmark for managing the crisis.

Both the IPCC and the World Bank reports run several scenarios that indicate what will likely occur if our efforts fall short, as they

online at http://www.worldbank.org/en/topic/climatechange/publication/turn-down-the-heat.

[3] *2014 Climate Change Adaptation Roadmap* (Washington, DC: U.S. Department of Defense, 2014). Available online at http://ppec.asme.org/wp-content/uploads/2014/10/CCARprint.pdf.

seem to be doing. Without aggressive mitigation, we are headed to an increase in temperature of 4 degrees Celsius by the end of the century. Under such circumstances, we can expect what they refer to as "devastating" scenarios: the inundation of coastal cities; increasing risks for food production . . . dry regions becoming dryer, wet regions wetter; unprecedented heat waves . . . substantially exacerbated water scarcity . . . increased intensity of tropical cyclones; and irreversible loss of biodiversity.[4]

In fact, the "irreversible loss of biodiversity" is well underway — not just from climate change but from the cumulative impact of human activity. Over the history of life on this planet there have been five major mass extinction events, when the number of species on the earth plummeted. The most recent and most famous, of course is the one that wiped out the dinosaurs. The causes of these events have been various — asteroids, vulcanism, ocean acidification — but all involved climate change too rapid for species to adapt. Biologists are now in broad agreement that we are actually in the early stages of a sixth major extinction event. Only this one is unique in that it will not have been caused by deep earth processes or an asteroid from outer space but by the impact of a single species — Homo sapiens.[5] But the truly bad news comes, not from biologists, but from oceanographers. We tend to think of the ocean as so vast that it must be exempt from the impact of human activity, but nothing could be further from the truth. Severe overfishing, agricultural run-off, chemical pollution, and coastal habitat destruction are interacting with the increasing acidification of the oceans from climate change, causing the collapse of oceanic ecological systems. That is not to say that there is nothing to be done, but as one scientist put it, "there is no easy fix. Hell, there isn't even a hard fix."[6] What we can hope to do does not fit under the word "fix."

When I accepted the invitation to do this lecture, I did not anticipate having to begin it this way. As I did my research, however, it became clear to me that to tell the truth I had to report some very disturbing things. And I could not put what I had learned into an

---

[4] *Turn Dowm the Heat*, Executive Summary, xvii–xxxv.

[5] Elizabeth Kolbert, *The Sixth Extinction: An Unnatural History* (New York: Henry Holt, 2014).

[6] Lisa-ann Gershwin, *Stung! On Jellyfish Blooms and the Future of the Ocean* (Chicago: University of Chicago Press, 2013), 340.

edifying story in which the human race, after blundering its way heedlessly toward the precipice, suddenly comes to its senses, turns away from its reckless course, and everything is saved. I certainly hope we do come to our senses and turn from our reckless course. There are reasons for being cautiously optimistic that we may. But everything will not be saved. The world that comes after this century will be very different from the one that existed before, much poorer in biodiversity, much less hospitable to many species. At the same time, I do not see the future in dystopian terms. And much of the reason I do not succumb to despair is because of having to think through our situation in theological terms and in particular through engagement with the profound wisdom of the biblical texts.

One might not think that the Bible, composed among peoples who literally could not imagine the human technological prowess of the industrial age that threatens the planet, would have much to say to this situation. But it does. Again and again, I am struck by the wisdom in these texts and their capacity to ground us in the truth and to disclose the hope in our situation. What I want to do at this point is to look at the theological anthropology of the biblical texts that can help us understand who we are, the images of an eschatological vision that can guide us, and the reassurance to be found in the faithfulness of the God of creation.

As I sat stunned and numb, after finally grasping the enormity of catastrophic changes that human activity is causing, I had a sense of self-estrangement. Who are we? Who are we as a species that we could be capable of doing this? And I meant that question in two senses—how is it that we have the *power* to do such damage? But also, how could we be so *foolish*? I went back to reread the Yahwist's creation story in Genesis 2–3, the "garden of Eden" story from the Pentateuchal source we call the Yahwist. I read it alongside books by physical anthropologists and geneticists who have also been reflecting on the origin of early humans. These two accounts turned out to be surprisingly mutually informative.

Genesis 2–3 is, after all—though the fundamentalists do not like to hear this—a story about human evolution, about the birth of our species and the consequences of that evolutionary development. While the Yahwist hadn't read Darwin, he was profoundly interested in the place of human beings in relation to animals on the one hand and to divine beings on the other. In that story, God first forms the creature that is to become the human, the 'adam, from the dust of the earth, from the 'adamah. And when God places the creature in the garden, there is one and only one stipulation—the creature may not eat from the tree of the knowledge of good and bad. These terms do not simply mean moral good and moral evil. Rather, they refer to the capacity to discriminate in any matter concerning what is good and bad. They refer to the capacity for rational, deliberative choice. As we later learn, this capacity to make deliberative choice is one of the things characteristic of divine beings—and whatever the 'adam is, it is not a divine being. In fact, the 'adam is simply what we would call "an animal." We realize this, because when it occurs to God that the creature might be lonely, God attempts to make a helper corresponding to it—and what does God make?—other animals and birds. From God's perspective the 'adam and the other animals are of the same nature—all of them made from the dust of the earth.

This is also what we discovered in scientific terms in the nineteenth century with the theory of evolution. Our ancestral species is that of the apes, which appear approximately 23 million years ago. The earliest hominid, Homo erectus, appears about 2 million years ago. And our own species, Homo sapiens, a bare 150,000 to 200,000 years ago.

In the Yahwist's imagination in Genesis 2, there were two kinds of beings in the world—animals and divine beings. By the end of Genesis 3 there will be three kinds of beings—animals, humans, and divine beings. How does this happen? As we know, it involves that tree of the knowledge of good and bad, the image that represents the capacity for rational discernment, rational deliberation. One of the Yahwist's profound perceptions is that this is a feature that does not characterize animals. Though we may have a slightly more nuanced view of animal cognition nowadays, the Yahwist's perception is basically correct. Animals are more "hard-wired" than are humans with all of the instincts that they need to live. They don't have to draw on rational processes in the same way that humans do. Animals don't need to create "culture" as humans do. They don't have or need the capacity for symbolic thought or develop language.

This capacity, says the Yahwist, is a characteristic of divine beings. As the wily talking snake, the trickster figure of the story, says to the woman, "as soon as you eat of [the fruit of the tree of knowledge] your eyes will be opened and you will be like divine beings who know good from bad" (Gen 3:4).[7] And when the human eat of it, what happens? It's a funny scene—"their eyes were opened and they saw . . . that they were naked" (Gen 3:7)! Now that hardly seems like divine knowledge. But it's a very shrewd observation. The term "naked" is one that cannot be used intelligibly of animals. One cannot intelligibly say that a deer or a lion is "naked." One can only use that term meaningfully of humans. The concept of nakedness is one of the sharpest dividing lines between humans and other animals. Why? Because our capacity for reflective self-consciousness, which underlies our sense of bodily self-consciousness and shame, is dependent upon the large and developed brains that humans uniquely have. What the Yahwist depicts in this economical image is the birth of the human as an animal who has somehow gotten hold of a divine characteristic—a complex cognitive capacity—and is no longer like the other animals. This is Homo sapiens.

But why does the story present this quality as something that was off-limits to us? Why did God not want us to have this capacity? Actually, the story is rather ambivalent about that—the tree was off-limits, but it was right there—within reach. And narratives of this type, that begin with a prohibition, have a plot structure that requires that the prohibition be breached. After all, the Yahwist was trying to explain how humans came to be the way they are. But the prohibition has a serious function in the story. This divine capacity was marked as off-limits to us because we are not, in fact, gods. We are not equipped to handle this capacity wisely. We are this anomalous creature. We are both splendid and very, very dangerous.

If we turn back from Genesis to the story of our evolution that anthropologists and geneticists have uncovered, our "Eden" was in Africa.[8] And, relevantly to our concern here today, the story of our evolutionary development was deeply connected with climate

---

[7] Unless otherwise noted, Scripture translations are those of the author.

[8] Several excellent books provide accessible summaries of the archaeological and genetic evidence for reconstructing early human development. See, for example, Ian Tattersall, *Masters of the Planet: The Search for Human Origins* (New York: St. Martin's Press, 2012); Sam Keen, *The Violinist's Thumb: And Other Lost Tales of Love, War, and Genius, as Written by Our Genetic Code* (New York: Little Brown, 2012), 203–25; Spencer Wells, *The Journey of Man: A Genetic Odyssey* (New York: Random House, 2002).

change—and more than once. Most relevant to our concern, around 70,000 years ago we nearly went extinct as a species. The problem was climate change—that time, likely induced by a super-volcano. Probably, there were no more than two thousand humans left in the world, perhaps even fewer. We would certainly have made the endangered species list. But we did survive. And going through the eye of this evolutionary needle was the catalyst of extraordinary change. Approximately 60,000 years ago there was not only a population explosion of humans but a geographical expansion into new territories. Not only did humans fan out within Africa but also out of Africa to Australia by 50,000 years ago, and by 20,000 years ago into the Middle East, to Asia, to Europe, and eventually to the Americas. Moreover, by 35,000 years ago humans were producing cave art of extraordinary beauty and sophistication and spiritual depth. And there is also evidence of music and intricate flint tools—and who knows what other arts. How can we look at this extraordinary development without tears of wonder that living creatures of any species could have self-consciousness, that they could be capable of speaking and singing and making art and experiencing spiritual awe. Truly, something godlike is here. These humans had eaten from the tree of knowledge, and who among us would wish that they had not?

Our more cynical friend the Yahwist, however, would remind us that this birth of the human—though truly marvelous—was not necessarily benign—certainly not for the earth itself. The Yahwist depicts God angrily confronting the first couple. God curses the woman with the pain of childbirth—a telling punishment, since it is the large brains and consequently large skulls of Homo sapiens that make human birthgiving so much more painful and dangerous than that of other animals. But even more chillingly, God says to the man "cursed be the earth on account of you." The Yahwist draws attention specifically to agriculture. Not only is it back-breaking work for humans, but in fact it often leaves the earth itself depleted and worn out, no longer yielding rich biodiversity but only "thorns and thistles" (Gen 3:17-19).

In the light of where we stand, it is hard to argue with the Yahwist. In fact, our "curse upon the earth" goes back even further. Even our upper Paleolithic hunter-gatherer ancestors played a large role in driving the megafauna of the early Holocene into extinction.

Wherever we went, the largest prey species disappeared, and consequently, the predators. But this was not a story of greed and foolishness—I wish that it were—for then we might learn our lesson. But we did not hunt these animals carelessly. It is simply that our cleverness made us far more efficient hunters than anything else these prey species had had to evolve to defend themselves against. They were unable to reproduce fast enough to meet the challenge we presented. We imposed change too rapidly. And that has been our story ever since. Our cleverness, so wonderful in and of itself, completely outpaced a world that had evolved to a different tempo. And the tempo of the changes we have wrought upon the earth has only increased, until in the past 250 years it has become unbearable for the earth. Two hundred and fifty years. Only a milisecond in evolutionary terms.

This is the profound irony of what the Yahwist saw. Such cleverness, such ability to distinguish between what's good and what's bad—can only be wielded wisely by divine beings who can look upon the whole vast nexus of causes and their effects. Humans see too narrowly and so make devastatingly bad decisions that look so good at the time. This is beyond "sin." This is a tragic structure in our very being.

Initially, the Yahwist seems to suggest that both good and bad results occur from this decisive change that brings the human into being. The first story, tellingly, is one of murder (Gen 4:1-16). But there are also accounts of the creation of the arts of civilization—of music, of cattle raising, of metallurgy, of city-founding, of the institution of religion itself (Gen 4:17-25). And yet, in his introduction to the flood story, our old cynic the Yahwist finally concludes that "every plan devised by the human mind was nothing but bad, all the time" (Gen 6:5). He gives a resoundingly negative evaluation to our rational capacity. The fact that this is his judgment on the cause of the flood, the mythic global eco-catastrophe, is chilling. What would he say to us today?

The Yahwist's cynicism is not the only voice that speaks about theological anthropology in Genesis. The Priestly voice that we hear in Genesis 1 is more confident that our remarkable difference from the other animals is not simply the result of an evolutionary experiment gone awry, but claims that this human creature with its capacity for reflective self-consciousness in the image and likeness of God is intended by God. This, of course, is the basis for that controversial command to human beings to "subdue the earth" and to exercise "dominion" over its creatures (Gen 1:26, 28). When I teach this passage in an environmental theology class, it is often a hard sell. Isn't the theology stemming from this passage the source of our distorted relationship with nature? Our sense that the earth is simply ours to use merely as "natural resources"? It is not difficult to find some disturbing interpretations of this passage to that effect in some of the irresponsible corners of the conservative blogosphere. Proper exegesis can easily demonstrate what is wrong with that interpretation. But that is not my focus here. My focus here is rather on the hard truth this passage does tell, a truth that I, along with many others, have not wanted to face. Human "subduing of the earth" and "dominion" is not an option that we can debate, a theology we can endorse or reject. It is a simple fact.

The typical debate over whether dominion can be interpreted in a benign fashion as "stewardship" or whether "subduing" and "dominion" point to a more antagonistic relationship is too simplistically framed. Our very presence on this earth has resulted and will continue to result in a diminishment of its pre-human biodiversity. Our presence subdues the earth. And yet, the preservation of the maximum possible biodiversity now depends upon our wise dominion, our decisions about the earth and its systems. One of the most disturbing realizations I had when reading Elizabeth Kolbert's *The Sixth Extinction*, was that the very things that make human beings distinctive—our inventiveness, our ability to flourish in a wide variety of environments—is itself incompatible with the kind of biodiversity that preceded us.[9] The incredible biodiversity on this planet is the product of separated environments and a very slow pace of the introduction of alien species. When the supercontinent Pangea broke up into distinct land masses, these new more isolated places became grand staging areas for evolutionary differentiation. In Australia, for example, there were no native placental mammals. So— what did nature do there? All the ecological niches that were elsewhere filled by placental mammals were filled in Australia by a riot of marsupials: big ones and little ones, carnivorous ones and herbivorous ones, nocturnal ones and diurnal ones. There was a creative

---

[9] Kolbert, *The Sixth Extinction*, 229–35.

explosion of marsupials. Although bats and rats introduced themselves into Australia without human intervention, all other placental mammals were brought, intentionally or inadvertently, by
humans—with devastating consequences. Many marsupial species
are now endangered, because they cannot compete with the introduced mammals and are otherwise losing habitat. Human beings,
that most migratory of species, have effectively knit all of the land
masses back together again into a super-continent. And the change
that has resulted from our presence is too fast for natural adaptation.

We have only recently begun to realize this and to recognize
what is required to allow healthy ecosystems with all their rich
biodiversity to flourish. And there are some very encouraging success stories where badly damaged ecosystems have been restored
through intentional human intervention.

Unlike the Yahwist, who merely gives a cynical shrug and denies
that humans are capable of changing, the Priestly writer's story of
the flood and its aftermath sees the possibility of a non destructive
future as humans orient themselves to the transcendence of divine
guidance as given in the law and the covenant (Gen 9:1-17). We are
not gods, and for that very reason need God.

Spending time with the theological anthropologies of the Bible
and reading them in conversation with scientific anthropologies
grounds us. It helps us think more clearly about ourselves as a species, our uniqueness that makes us both wonderful and dangerous,
and how we must orient ourselves to the transcendent if we are to be
a blessing and not a curse upon the earth.

But right now, we find ourselves in a crisis. If catastrophe is to be
averted, we must act with great speed, with an urgency and a deci-
siveness that has, so far, eluded us. It is a time of great anxiety, great
conflict, great uncertainty. For this, too, the Bible offers important
conversation partners. In particular, I am thinking about the way in
which the Bible deals with the relation of human action, divine
intentionality, and the nature of time itself. Much of the Bible, especially the Hebrew Bible, tells a long narrative story. It begins with
the accounts of the Priestly Writer and the Yahwist. And the rest of
the story from Genesis through 2 Kings might be read as a working
out of these authors' "bets" about the nature of humanity. Since
much of the story is contained in the Deuteronomistic History that
runs from Joshua through 2 Kings, I call this Deuteronomistic time.

Deuteronomistic time is structured according to the working out of actions and their consequences. It's real world time. It's political time. It's the time of success or failure. It's the time of taking responsibility for one's actions. Its temporal horizons are relatively short—but they are intergenerational. Truly, the actions of the parents have consequences for the lives of their children.

Our time of response to the crisis of the climate feels very much like Deuteronomistic time. It is a time in which we are waking up to the consequences of our actions, to the ways in which the choices of older generations are being visited on the lives of the coming generations. It is a time in which we realize that we have been enchanted by the idols of our own making—our unprecedented technological prowess that truly seems like the actions of beings who have become "like gods." And we are being called to account by prophetic voices who demand that we look at the consequences of our idolatry.

Deuteronomistic time is a time of intensity and focus, a purposeful time, but it is also a heavy time. It is a time in which both success and failure are possible, and thus it is a time of judgment. What we do will be judged. It will be judged by the objective judgment of our climate itself, by the judgment of the coming generations who will either praise us for acting courageously or curse us for blithely stumbling into catastrophe, and by the judgment of God on how we have carried out our task of dominion. It is easy to find oneself mentally and spiritually exhausted by the sense of responsibility, the fear of failure, the anxiety about the future.

But Deuteronomistic time is not the only time. I find both comfort and hope, perhaps surprisingly, in eschatological time, apocalyptic time. When I first began to teach on the Bible and environmentalism, apocalyptic eschatology was the topic I dreaded. This was the one thing in the biblical corpus that seemed unredeemably anti-environmental. "For I am about to create new heavens and a new earth; the former things shall not be remembered or come to mind" (Isa 65:17). "Then I saw a new heaven and a new earth; for the first heaven and the first earth had passed away" (Rev 21:1). Wasn't this a biblical vision of a "disposable world"? That was hardly the model I was looking for!

The more I have lived with the conversation between the Bible and environmental concerns, however, the more I have come to see how vitally important is the perspective on time that is embodied in apocalyptic eschatology. Not surprisingly, apocalyptic eschatology emerged in the centuries after the fall of Judah and the Exile, in the difficult time of "living after" a crisis that was not only national and political but also spiritual and religious. It was a way of thinking about time, divine intentionality, and human responsibility that grasped the limitations of purely Deuteronomistic time, though it did not reject it entirely. Apocalyptic eschatology is not about evading or escaping our responsibilities. It incorporates what I have called Deuteronomistic time into its moral vision. But it places Deuteronomistic time within a much, much broader story—the story of creation from its very beginnings until its ultimate end. This is not time on a human scale, as Deuteronomistic time is, but time on a divine scale—deep time, cosmic time. It understands time as divided into a succession of great ages and epochs, stretching immeasurably beyond the scope of a few human generations.

One of the Dead Sea Scrolls speaks of "the ages of old" reaching back to creation and forward to the eschaton. It speaks of "the earth with all that springs from it, the seas and the deeps, [according to] all the plans for them for all the eternal epochs." The hymn acknowledges God's role ("[who] established them from ages of old") and speaks of the role and purpose of these ages and the creatures that inhabit them ("that they might make known your glory in all your dominion," 1QH 5.26-29). But the image of this deep time is not simply of one age gradually passing into the next. No, it is a story of endings and new beginnings, of the destruction of what was of old, the creation of new things that will be after them, all of this comprehended by the invincible wisdom of God.

I was struck by the analogy between this perception of time and what the geologists call "deep time," that is, the time of the great epochs of the earth's history—the Cambrian, the Ordovician, the Silurian, the Devonian, the Carboniferous, the Permian, the Triassic, the Jurassic, the Cretaceous, the Paleogene, the Quaternary—and now, perhaps, the Anthropocene. This scientific deep time was only recognized in the nineteenth century with the understanding of geologic processes and a comprehension of what the fossils of extinct plants and animals represented. It was a recognition there was a time when these astonishing creatures—and not us—dominated the planet. And with each successive age a different repertoire of plants and animals flourished. There was a time before flowering plants, a time before mammals, a time before dinosaurs, a time before reptiles, a time before there were any land animals, any land plants. Geologists have documented the five mass extinction events in earth's history but have noted that as each is an ending, so it is a beginning, or as that Dead Sea Scroll prayer speaks of such transitions, "destroying what was of old, creating new things" (1QH 5.29). Extinction events are also recognized as evolutionary gateways, opportunities for nature to experiment with new forms of life.[10] Although the apocalyptic theologians were predeterministic in a way that geologists are certainly not, they would have grasped what the geologists perceived, and understood it to be part of what they described as the *raz nihyeh*, the mystery of what was, and is, and is to be. Or, as we might put it in terms of Christian theology, the mystery of God, "the Alpha and the Omega." To think in Trinitarian terms, God as the holy spirit who infuses all creation, can take even a time of chaotic desolation at the end of an era and make from it a new and glorious world.

Apocalyptic time does not take away our responsibility, our answerability for our actions. It will not take away our guilt before God and the rest of creation if we bring about a mass extinction. It will not make our grief and our shame at the destruction we have caused any less. But by contextualizing our actions within a much larger story, it saves us from despair and apathy and frees us from paralyzing anxiety. It allows us to trust that God is present in this world, and that even if we fail, God will take the debris of our failure and continue to create a world of new beauty and wonder that will in its own way declare the glory of God.

But there is one more word of comfort and encouragement that I see in apocalyptic eschatology, namely in the way it envisions the healing of a damaged and depleted world. In our despair over human impact on the world it is easy to imagine that the only hope for wholeness for the earth is for humans no longer to be part of it. Or for us once again to become like the other animals, that is to say, to return to an Eden before the Fall. But that is not the imagery of biblical eschatology. The key images in biblical eschatology provocatively

---

[10] Tim F. Flannery, *The Weather Makers: How Man Is Changing the Climate and What It Means for Life on Earth* (New York: Grove Press, 2001), 45–53.

combine imagery of Eden with, of all things, the image of the city. We often think of the city as the symbol of all that is wrong with human ways of being—the image of our fall into anthropocentrism. But as we envision a transformed future for our planet, a healing future, it will not help to think in terms of romanticized nostalgia, a return to some pure hunter-gatherer past. That is why I find the imagery of apocalyptic eschatology so intriguing. This image first appears in the book of Ezekiel, written after the Exile. He is shown an urban setting, a temple constructed on a high mountain. And from that temple flows a river. And as that river flows to the east, through the dryness of the Judean wilderness, it brings life. "Everything will live where the river goes." Trees flourish on its banks, and its waters even transform the stagnant Dead Sea into fresh water. Where nothing lived, now there will be many fish. "And on the banks, on both sides of the river, there will grow all kinds of trees for food. Their leaves will not wither nor their fruit fail. . . . Their fruit will be for food, and their leaves for healing" (Ezek 47:1-12). In this eschatological vision of a new Eden, the city is no longer the sign of our fallenness, but because it is the place where God dwells, it becomes the source of the healing of the land. The book of Revelation picks up this image and develops it in Revelation 21–22. For John, the New Jerusalem is an open city whose gates are never shut, and the river of life flows through its very streets. The tree of life is there, producing fruit abundantly at all seasons and healing the nations with its leaves.

These are evocative images, not simple depictions of some imagined future. But as eschatological images they disclose in symbolic form some not yet realized possibility. They suggest a way in which we may be drawn in hope and faith toward a future in which our transformed cities become not a place away from nature but the site where we practice the ecological wholeness that is the foretaste of a redeemed and reconciled world. Though there is much in our situation that makes us anxious, the theological resources of our tradition offer us ways of living with understanding of who we are, with seriousness of purpose, and yet with the humility that our actions—whether successful or not—are enfolded in a process that will incorporate them into the larger story of divine faithfulness to creation.

CHAPTER 12

"Fish of Every Kind": The Kingdom of God and Global Pluralism

Jehu J. Hanciles

Centennial Academic Conference Lecture
March 20, 2015

Foresight is the secret ingredient of success.[1]

In February 1966, *Time* magazine published an article titled "Looking Toward A.D. 2000" that included a range of predictions from various academic and scientific disciplines about the near future—all of which added up to a remarkable vision centered on the year 2000.[2] Some, like the speculation that by that year many people would stay at home, doing their work via countrywide telecommunication, now appear reasonably prescient. But most of the "scientific" forecasts pronounced back then, with unbridled optimism by professionals in various fields, would be greeted with incredulous amusement today. These include the confident assertions that by 2000 both the automobile and the highway would be obsolete, giving way to hovercraft that ride on air; that bacterial and viral diseases would have been virtually wiped out; that memory loss accompanying senility would be eliminated. Also, that use of drugs to control personality would be widely accepted—such that "if a wife or husband seems to be unusually grouchy on a given evening a . . . spouse will be able to pop down to the corner drugstore, buy some anti-grouch pills, and slip them into the coffee."

The article captured the new-found confidence that "Western man," as one observer put it, is "not trapped in an absurd fate

---

[1] Edward Cornish, "The Search for Foresight: How the Futurist was Born," *The Futurist*, 41, no. 1, (January-February, 2007): 52.

[2] "The Futurists: Looking Toward A.D. 2000," *Time*, February 25, 1966.

but . . . can and must choose his destiny—a technological reasser-tion of free will." The year of publication (1966) also marked the founding of the World Future Society, an organization partly in-spired by the conviction that "the study of the future might help the cause of world peace" and "offer a kind of counterweight to the bur-den of traditional grievances and present fears."[3] In the space of a year, the organization had 1,500 members (or "futurists," as they be-came known), a third of whom were "university professors or other-wise engaged in higher education."[4] The obsession with the future quickly became a growth industry, attracting millions of dollars in research funding. As Edward Cornish, founder of the World Future Society, recalled some four decades later:

> I began to see the future not as a totally impenetrable realm about which we can know absolutely nothing, but rather as an exciting frontier, offering enormous possibilities but also ex-traordinary dangers. We cannot possibly know everything that lies ahead, but with effort we can glimpse the possibilities of our future. . . . Foresight is the secret ingredient of success.[5]

At a centennial milestone such as we are now commemorating at Candler, it is only natural that we celebrate how far we have come (our growth and transformation), take stock of who we are (our identity), and assess what to strive for as we move forward (our "imagined future"). These three elements are, of course, intercon-nected, and all require deep theological awareness—but by far the most challenging is how we assess the future.

As a historian, this leaves me with a handicap, for I have more experience with reflecting on the past than with predicting the fu-ture. Indeed, given the fact that, generally speaking, academics and

---

[3] Cornish, "The Search for Foresight: How the Futurist was Born," 53. In 2014, it claimed to have "members in more than 80 countries around the world."

[4] Edward Cornish, "The Search for Foresight: The World Future Society's Emergence from Dream to Reality," *The Futurist* 41, no. 2 (March-April, 2007): 42. By 1987, its twenty-three thousand members included "many churchmen, clergy, theologians, missionaries, mission executives, and even a number of missiologists." See David B. Barrett, "Forecasting the Future in World Mission: Some Future Faces of Missions," *Missiology* 15, no. 4 (1987): 434.

[5] Cornish, "The Search for Foresight: How the Futurist was Born," 52.

other professionals have a dismal track record for making accurate forecasts about trends in their respective fields, my instinct as a historian is to uncover such imprudence, not to participate in it. Perhaps historians are particularly resistant to the seductive allure of postulating an imagined future, in part because, for historians at least, such a future must of necessity take the form of a new era in which the lessons of history are fully learned and rigorously applied—a feat of extraordinary human achievement that would then make history somewhat redundant and create mass unemployment for historians! Until such a time, the problem with the future is that it can look remarkably like the past in important respects, and present realities only imperfectly reveal the promise of the future. Hence the need for "prophetic discernment" and unrelenting theological enquiry.

The vision of the future that animated the best minds in the 1960s, and long after, was marked by two striking omissions. First, the lack of a global perspective was epitomized by the almost complete silence on non-Western societies or experiences. In the *Time* magazine essay, the sole reference to the non-Western world reflected concern about the possible failure of underdeveloped countries to catch up with the dazzling future imagined by leading scientific experts of the day. The future that captivated their minds was an exclusively Western one, centered on the experiences of "Western man." Many pinned their hopes on the prospects of "an increasingly homogenized world culture" (based on Western ideals) to generate international harmony or world peace. There was no place in this singular vision for the messy, conflictual, irrepressible diversity that was and remains intrinsic to the human condition. The Western faith in progress was also a faith in Western preeminence. The ideals, values, and models that defined the new world order were Western and it stood to reason that the non-Western world would partake in the same package of progress and prosperity only insofar as it adopted the measures that guaranteed this outcome. The acute dichotomies of the Cold War period encouraged stark choices. When the future of the world—indeed of human kind—is reduced to two alternatives, global pluralism gets little attention.

The second major omission from the futurist vision was religion or, perhaps more accurately, religious existence. In the 1960s prognostications (or visions) of a world increasingly freed from the vexing inconvenience of religious claims and ideals enjoyed

137

ascendency. In his bestselling book, *The Secular City*, published the previous year (1965), Harvey Cox, an American Baptist minister and Harvard professor, proclaimed the unstoppable spread of secularism and the end of religion in the modern world.[6] This outlook was not entirely baseless. Partly due to the rise of communism and the impact of two world wars, the proportion of religious people in the world showed significant decline in the decades leading up to 1960.[7]

To be sure, the picture was mixed. In many parts of Europe and North America, religious identity and church allegiance remained potent elements in political and social life—as the bitter Protestant-Catholic conflict in Northern Ireland and religion-inspired resistance to communism in countries like Poland clearly indicated.[8] The growth of Pentecostalism also remained untrammeled. But much of Western Europe had entered a post-Christendom phase. Even American Christianity, for all its vibrancy, was experiencing declining influence in public or national life. Moreover, decolonization and the closing of China had fueled widespread backlash against Western missions and further discredited the Christendom framework. Only much later would it become manifest that the rising commitment to the global spread of Western liberal democracy, principally through development schemes and NGOs, replaced one form of imperialism with another.[9]

In the event, Western secularism was arguably at its most assertive. The futurist vision was shaped by the conviction that Western man "has regained his nerve" and has come to believe, rightly, that he can accomplish anything.[10] Two months after the publication of the article under discussion, the cover of *Time* magazine (April 1966)

---

[6] Harvey Cox, *The Secular City* (New York: Macmillan, 1965; 25th anniversary ed. New York: Collier Books, 1990).

[7] Between 1910 and 1970, the number of people in the world estimated to be non-religious (atheists and agnostics) rose from around 3 million (0.2 percent) to almost 700 million (18.9 percent). Todd M. Johnson, "Global Religious Trends: Implications for U.S. Foreign Policy," *The Review of Faith & International Affairs* 6, no. 3 (Fall, 2008): 43–45.

[8] David Reynolds, *One World Divisible: A Global History Since 1945* (New York: W. W. Norton, 2000), 231–34.

[9] For a brief but penetrating comment, see "Sins of the Secular Missionaries," *The Economist* (2000): 25–27.

[10] My hunch," opined Emmanuel Mesthene (d. 1990), then executive director of the multimillion dollar Harvard Program on Technology and

presented the issue to the reading public starkly and profoundly with a three-word headline: "Is God Dead?"[11]

To a large extent, these two issues, devaluation of non-Western experiences and rising confidence in a secular future, reflected the new triumphalism that became prominent among the Western intellectual class in the early Cold War era. The two issues were also tied in a less apparent, more philosophical, way. Religious systems and non-Western societies were marked by a pluralism and implacable diversity that were at odds with the vision of a homogenous world order produced by the benefits of scientific progress and the spread of economic modernization.[12] Belief in the superior gains of homogenized human existence (a uniquely Western ideal) means that religious or cultural pluralism is often viewed as an unhelpful predicament and a problem to be solved. Pluralism is inherently unpredictable; homogeneity less so.

Today, it is easy to see how things have turned out quite differently than they were imagined half a century ago; especially as regards religious existence and the significance of non-Western experiences or realities within the new global order. But, while it is obvious that the world we live in today is radically different in important ways from the one envisaged by many leading minds half a century ago, this is not to say that the assumptions and priorities that undergirded their predictions have also changed. If how we imagine the future is inseparable from how we understand the present, then what we consider important in contemporary existence provides the clearest indication of the imperatives that frame our priorities and expectations. It therefore says something about

---

Society, "is that man may have finally expiated his original sin, and might now aspire to bliss." Quoted in "The Futurists: Looking Toward A.D. 2000,"*Time* (February 25, 1966).

[11] In 1968, two years later, renowned American sociologist, Peter Berger told the *New York Times* that by the twenty-first century, "religious believers are likely to be found only in small sects, huddled together to resist a world-wide secular culture." See Toby Lester, "Oh, Gods!" *Atlantic Monthly* (February, 2002): 39.

[12] It is worth noting that the Western encounter with the enormous diversity of non-Western societies in the sixteenth to nineteenth centuries led to the creation of such new scientific disciplines as linguistics and anthropology.

our vision and purpose as a theological institution devoted to serving the worldwide Christian community that we have identified global pluralism (as it relates to the "kingdom of God") as a key issue of our time; indeed, of this century.

Global pluralism, as I understand it, infers an understanding that the global order comprises a vast array of independent (but interconnected) strands—languages, cultures, nationalities, societies and ethnicities—that also reflect the diversity of our human family. As a concept, it also registers implicit rejection of the modern notion of a single global culture, or global homogenization. This is not to suggest a static condition—the number of world's spoken languages has been declining for centuries (and with them unique forms of cultural expression and identity)[13] while new religious forms constantly materialize.

What is unique about contemporary experience is the degree to which global interconnectedness and interdependence—facilitated by extraordinary advances in technologies of communication and travel—have vastly increased the scale of interaction between diverse human populations. Thus, the same processes of globalization that contribute to the marginalization or extinction of languages also provide the means to preserve them for posterity and, paradoxically, enable even the most obscure language to be shared worldwide. Yet, the dynamics of globalization also mean that, rather than the emergence of a "world language" (as long assumed), multilingualism will become increasingly manifest and widespread.[14] The rest of this presentation examines global pluralism as a critical issue of our day and explores how this relates to the "kingdom of God." This biblical concept that evokes God's presence and saving power and furnishes us with important insights as we grapple with new realities.

---

[13] Almost half of the existing six thousand to seven thousand languages in the world are expected to become extinct in the next century. Stephen R. Anderson, *How Many Languages Are There in the World?* (Washington, DC: Linguistic Society of America, 2010), 2.

[14] Stefan Lovgren, "English in Decline as a First Language, Study Says," *National Geographic News* (February 26, 2004); Barbara Wallraff, "What Global Language?," *The Atlantic Monthly* (November, 2000).

Global Pluralism in Biblical Perspective: The Babel Story

The tendency to view the immeasurable diversity that character-izes human existence as an unhelpful predicament has a long his-tory and remains prevalent among Christians of various stripes. This much is indicated by the traditional interpretation of the "Ba-bel" episode recorded in Genesis 11, a striking narrative that seeks to illuminate human origin and arguably marks the climax of the cre-ation story.[15]

Throughout the history of the Christian church down to the present day, interpretation of the Babel story has been dominated by the "pride and punishment" tradition.[16] In this understanding, the story describes the ungodly spirit evident in the actions or ambitions of a group of migrants who settle in Babylon (Mesopotamia). In defi-ance of God's explicit post-flood command that humans "increase . . . and fill the earth" (Gen 9:1, 7), this group decides to settle in one place and build a permanent, self-contained, city with a humongous tower. The assumption that this project reflects human hubris or sin-ful rebellion is based on their self-proclaimed desire to build "a tower that reaches to the heavens" and "make a name for ourselves" (Gen 11:4). Based on this perspective, the divine intention at creation was a culturally homogenous human population, speaking one lan-guage and occupying a single location. As such, the diversity of hu-man existence is a needless evil inflicted on humanity by a displeased deity in response to an act of prideful rebellion by our primeval ancestors. In other words, the extraordinary cultural plu-ralism that marks the human condition is a contravention of the ideal—a hallmark of divine disfavor.

The durability of the "pride and punishment" interpretative tra-dition belies apparent weaknesses. Taken in context, the condition of having the same language and location was not of the builders'

---

[15] E. J. van Wolde, *Words Become Worlds: Semantic Studies of Genesis 1-11* (New York: E.J. Brill, 1994), 105; Bernhard W. Anderson, *From Creation to New Creation: Old Testament Perspectives* (Minneapolis: Fortress, 1994), 167.

[16] See Theodore Hiebert, "The Tower of Babel and the Origin of the World's Cultures," *Journal of Biblical Literature* 126/1 (2007): 29–30; Theodore Hiebert, "Introduction," in *Toppling the Tower: Essays on Babel and Diversity*, ed. Hiebert (Chicago: McCormick Theological Seminary, 2004), 1–11.

making but rather "the earth's original situation."[17] Similarly, "a name for ourselves" more likely reflects the group's determination to preserve its unity and unique identity (epitomized by one language). The erection of a tower, in fact, is inconsequential, since towers were a common feature of religious structures in the ancient Mesopo- tamian world.[18] In short, the decision to build a city reflected decidedly human concerns for stable settled existence in the face of the unsettling and often jarring coexistence necessitated by migration. The builders' action, in other words, was prompted not by sinful rebellion but rather a natural human resistance to migration and the forces of dispersion—in their own words, "lest we be scattered abroad on the face of the earth" (Gen 11:4, KJV).

The building initiative, in effect, was rooted in the fear of losing cultural homogeneity and tribal identity. All this is to say that the divine response in this story is corrective not retributive. In fact, the clash of intentions, between the human intention and divine purpose, is embedded in the story line. There is more than a subtle hint in the narrative details to perennial tensions in humanity's social existence: preservation versus propagation; tribalism versus pluralism; singularity versus multiplicity. Perhaps the sharpest contrast, from a theological point of view, is between the builders' self-preoccupation ("for ourselves," Gen 11:4) and the divine purview ("the whole earth," Gen 11:9).[19]

Based on this reading of the text, the divine plan for humanity is not one language but a plurality of languages, not one location but global dispersion, not a single name or cultural identity but a multiplicity of cultures. The Babel story, then, teaches that the plurality of languages, peoples, and nationalities dispersed throughout the world reflects not divine punishment but divine purpose. That this central truth mattered to the ancients is striking, since linguistic

---

[17] Van Wolde, *Words Become Worlds*, 98.

[18] Indeed, the phrase "a tower that reaches to the heavens" was a popular cliché in the ancient Near East for "impressive height," and it "appears often in descriptions of fortifications and cultic installations" which typically include towers. Hiebert, "The Tower of Babel and the Origin of the World's Cultures," 35 (see notes), 37–38.

[19] Van Wolde, *Words Become Worlds*, 95–96, notes that the catchphrase "the whole earth" brackets the story and provides a critical reference point for both human action and the divine response.

diversity was even greater in the ancient world than it is today.[20] Down through the ages, the hostility and tensions between migrants and settled groups, foreigners and native populations, outsiders and mainstream societies, have been a dominant and recurrent theme of human existence. It is etched in the entire biblical narrative and exemplified by the cross-cultural expansion of the Christian movement down to the present day. But, as we shall see, it also finds explicit expression in the biblical conception of "the kingdom of God."

Migration and Global Pluralism

Crucially, the Babel story also affirms the basic historical fact that human migration is integral to global pluralism—especially as this applies to cultural diversity, the multiplicity of religious systems, and the vast array of political structures formed by distinctive societies. The history of humans is one of migration. Migration has been a constant feature of human existence, embedded in the complex transformations that shape our world. The migrant impulse has aided human evolution and has played an indispensable role in human development throughout the ages. It is not only a driving force of global pluralism, it is also instrumental in the cross-cultural encounters that intensify our consciousness of identity and difference.

Such is the extraordinary volume and velocity of migration in the present era that there are good grounds for calling it "the age of migration."[21] However, this recognition should not obscure the decided constraints that mark current migratory flows. Due to advancements in technologies of travel, the reach and rate of migrant movement has never been greater. At the same time, efforts to control or regulate cross-border movement have expanded tremendously. Consequently, compared to a hundred years ago, people are

---

[20] Until multicultural empires facilitated use of a lingua franca, "most people . . . could not communicate with those living across borders." Michael C. Howard, *Transnationalism in Ancient and Medieval Societies: The Role of Cross-Border Trade and Travel* (Jefferson, NC: McFarland, 2012), Kindle Locations 375–78.

[21] Stephen Castles and Mark J. Miller, *The Age of Migration: International Population Movements in the Modern World*, 4th ed. (New York: Guilford Press, 2009).

generally less free to migrate, as the great tide of unauthorized migrants indicates.

That said, there is no gainsaying the fact that global migratory flows have never been as extensive or unrelenting. By 2013, according to United Nations estimates, there were 232 million international migrants (people living outside their country of birth) in the world—the highest number of people living abroad in recorded history.[22] The majority of international migrants (136 million or 58.6 percent) lived in the North; Europe and North America are home to more than half (54 percent).[23]

With some 46 million international migrants, the United States has the highest of any country (19.8 percent); more than the next four (Russian Federation, Germany, Saudi Arabia, and the United Kingdom) combined.[24] America's new immigrants have transformed the nation into an icon of cultural pluralism. The first amendment guarantee of "the free exercise of religion" means that the ideal of religious pluralism has long been enshrined in the American experiment. But national consciousness has typically lagged well behind this ideal. A century ago, about the time when Candler came into existence, the massive influx of Roman Catholic immigrants had triggered an intensely hostile backlash.[25] To that generation present realities would have been utterly unimaginable. Indeed, as recently as 1960 the majority of immigrants in the

---

[22] "The Number of International Migrants Worldwide Reaches 232 Million," *Population Facts* 2 (2013): 1.

[23] Between 1990 and 2013, the number of international migrants worldwide rose by 50 percent" (over 77 million). *International Migration Report 2013* (New York: United Nations, Department of Economic and Social Affairs, Population Division, 2013), 1. Also, 232 million international migrants represent 3.2 percent of the world population. If they all lived in the same place, that place would be the world's fifth-largest country.

[24] "The Number of International Migrants Worldwide Reaches 232 Million," 2.

[25] In the late nineteenth century the typical American immigrant was described as "a European peasant, whose horizon has been narrow, whose moral and religious training has been meagre or false, and whose ideas of life are low," and also likely to "belong to the pauper and criminal classes." Josiah Strong, *Our Country: Its Possible Future and its Present Crisis* (New York: Baker & Taylor Co., 1885; rev. ed. 1891), 55f.

United States were from Canada, Germany, and Italy.[26] Half a century later, the picture is radically different. The overwhelming majority of the current waves of immigrants are nonwhite and come from more than 150 countries.[27] As a result, American society is now marked by a degree of pluralism that is unprecedented in its history. The transformative impact is even more startling. By 2050, according to the US Census Bureau, non-Hispanic whites will cease to be a majority, accounting for only 46 percent of the American population. There will be no single majority group in the country as a whole, and the majority of Americans will identify themselves as Hispanic, black, Asian, American Indian, Native Hawaiian, or Pacific Islander.[28]

The massive influx (and extraordinary growth) of nonwhite immigrant communities in the last three to four decades has vastly expanded cultural difference in Western societies and transformed Western metropolises. Many Western cities or capitals—London, New York, Sydney, Toronto, and Hamburg among them—are now characterized by "hyperdiversity," a term used to indicate that the diverse composition of the population is such that no single country of origin accounts for more than 25 percent of the immigrant stock.[29] In London, for instance, 42 percent of the workforce is foreign-born and school children speak more than three hundred languages;[30] whereas in New York City, "native born whites and

---

[26] Furthermore, no single country accounted for more than 15 percent of the total immigrant population. See Chiamaka Nwosu, Jeanne Batalova, and Gregory Auclair, *Frequently Requested Statistics on Immigrants and Immigration in the United States* (Washinton, DC: Migration Policy Institute, 2014). Slightly more than half (52 percent) come from Latin America and the Caribbean, and nearly a third (29 percent) come from Asia and the Middle East.

[27] Rubén G. Rumbaut and Alejandro Portes, "Ethnogenesis: Coming of Age in Immigrant America," in *Ethnicities: Children of Immigrants in America*, ed. Rumbaut and Portes (Berkeley: University of California Press, 2001), 9.

[28] Michael Cooper, "Census Officials, Citing Increasing Diversity, Say U.S. Will Be a 'Plurality Nation'," *New York Times* (December 12, 2012).

[29] Marie Price and Lisa Benton-Short, "Counting Immigrants in Cities across the Globe," *Migration Information Source* (January, 2007).

[30] Geoff Mulgan, "Feedback and Belonging: Explaining the Dynamics of Diversity," *Migration Information Source* (2009).

native-born parents make up only 20 percent" of the population and more than eight hundred languages are spoken daily.[31]

The Religious Dimension

The correlation between escalating migrant movements and the intensification of global pluralism has never been more evident, especially in connection with religious existence. In a striking refutation of the secularist vision, we live in a decidedly religious world. By 2010, 84 percent of the world's population was religiously affiliated; with a projected rise to 90 percent by 2020.[32] Importantly, the global religious landscape mirrors critical changes associated with wider processes of globalization, including the largely uninhibited flow of ideas, large-scale migrations and diaspora networks, as well as shifts in demographic representation that tend to pluralize centers of power.[33] In essence, globalization is not only helping to make our world more religious it is also transforming the nature of religion. In particular, processes of globalization have greatly enhanced the reach and potential of religious diasporas associated with all major religions. Writes Scott Thomas:

> The major world religions are all taking advantage of the opportunities provided by globalization to transform their messages and reach a new global audience. . . . Ethnic and religious diasporas in the global South are connected to the West in ways that can create or reinvigorate collective identities, whose influence can both promote social welfare and fuel terrorism and interreligious conflict. As a result, understanding religions worldwide—their beliefs, values, and practices and the way they influence the political goals, actions, and motivations of states and religious communities—will be an important task for

---

[31] Philip Kasinitz, John Mollenkopf, and Mary C. Water, "Becoming American/Becoming New Yorkers: The Second Generation in a Majority Minority City, *Migration Information Source* (October, 2006).

[32] *The Global Religious Landscape: A Report on the Size and Distribution of the World's Major Religious Groups as of 2010* (Pew Research Center, 2012), 9; *Christianity in its Global Context, 1970–2020* (Center for the Study of Global Christianity, 2013), 6.

[33] For a brief analysis, see Scott M. Thomas, "A Globalized God," *Foreign Affairs* 89/6 (November/December, 2010): 93–101.

U.S. and international foreign-policy makers in the coming decades.[34]

At the very least, this assessment confirms that the intersections between the Western and non-Western worlds are no longer restricted to Western initiatives, priorities, or ambitions. It also suggests that the unprecedented capacity for non-Western initiatives, ideas, and projects to impact Western societies is largely linked to global migratory flows.

Due to large-scale immigration from Asia and Africa, in particular, all the major religions are heavily represented among the new immigrant groups, and the dynamic religious diversity that now prevails in the metropolises of Western nations showcases the impact of those religions on society. Vociferous anti-immigration sentiments that depict immigration as a problem and immigrants as a threat have left many immigrant groups deeply alienated or socially marginalized. In Europe at least, experiments in multiculturalism have given way to loud calls for integration. But the fact remains that diaspora populations represent a focal point of cross-cultural contact and interaction.

New religious movements fostered by immigration typically experience a two-way conversion process: adaptation to highly secularized Western cultures introduces important modifications in their precepts and practice, but this process of indigenization increases their capacity to apply their beliefs and spirituality to Western concerns and attract new converts. The presence of large communities of Muslims, Christians, Buddhists, Hindus, etc., in Western contexts provides more occasions for contact and interaction at both the relational and societal levels than was the case for Western missions in non-Western contexts during the colonial era. In short, the dramatic rise of immigrant communities drawn from Asia and Africa means that Western societies, taken as a whole, increasingly represent notable sites of global pluralism in the present era. This has huge implications for religious encounter and exchange.

A 1991 study of converts to Islam in Britain found that 94 percent came from Christian backgrounds (73 percent from the Church of

---

[34] Ibid., 101.

England).[35] In the United States, American converts or American-born Muslims account for 25 to 30 percent of the Muslim population.[36] The majority of American converts to Islam are African American, for whom the embrace of Islam extends beyond personal faith to social and political considerations. But converts also include hundreds of thousands of white Americans whose adoption of Islam "has largely been mediated through immigrants from the Muslim world and their literature and institutions."[37]

Asia, birthplace of the most significant religious systems in the world, is a leading emitter of highly influential religio-cultural movements (such as New Age, Feng Shui, and the Hare Krishna movement) that have impacted modern Western society extensively. It is also a prominent source of the migrant movements that have produced a dramatic rise in Muslim, Hindu, and Buddhist populations—with members belonging to various strands of each faith—in the Western world. The presence and growth of Hinduism in the United States is strongly linked to immigration from India.[38] Between 1992 and 2012, the United States "admitted nearly a million Hindu immigrants," and by 2010, the total American

[35] Colin Chapman, *Islam and the West: Conflict, Coexistence or Conversion?* (Carlisle, England: Paternoster, 1998), 60–61. Chapman cites disillusionment with faiths such as Christianity or Judaism and disillusionment with Western society as being among the major reasons which contribute to conversion (pp. 61–73).

[36] M. A. Muqtedar Khan, "Constructing the American Muslim Community," in *Religion and Immigration: Christian, Jewish, and Muslim Experiences in the United States,* ed. Yvonne Yazbeck Haddad, Jane I. Smith, and John L. Esposito (Walnut Creek, CA: AltaMira Press, 2003), 176.

[37] Marcia Hermansen, "Conversion to Islam in Theological and Historical Perspectives," in *The Oxford Handbook of Religious Conversion,* ed. Lewis R. Rambo and Charles E. Farhadian (New York: Oxford University Press, 2014), 549. In his 1992 study, Larry Poston found that over 60 percent of American converts to Islam are male and the average age at the time of conversion was 29. Larry Poston, *Islamic da'wah in the West: Muslim Missionary Activity and the Dynamics of Conversion to Islam* (New York: Oxford University Press, 1992), 164, 166.

[38] Pew reports that "the great majority of Hindu immigrants come from India and neighboring countries with significant Hindu populations, such as Nepal and Bhutan." *The Religious Affiliation of U.S. Immigrants: Majority Christian, Rising Share of Other Faiths* (Washington, DC: Pew Research Center, 2013).

Hindu population was estimated at about 1.8 million.[39] The largest Hindu temple of any kind outside India is the BAPS Shri Swaminarayan Mandir located in Lilburn, Georgia (inaugurated in August 2007). But Hinduism is not a proselytizing faith. Its growth remains largely tied to immigrant influx and its impact lies primarily in adding to a vigorous pluralism and contributing to the body of religious ideas and practices that increasingly shape spiritual consciousness and aspirations in Western societies.

The spread of Buddhism to the West has also been greatly aided by massive immigrations from Asia, mainly from China and Japan. Immigrant Buddhism tends to be inward looking, but geopolitical events, such as the exile of the Dalai Lama and the migration of some Buddhist masters to the West with a missionary purpose, have elicited mainstream interest in the religion.[40] One of the largest Buddhist temples in North America, is located in Los Angeles and goes by the name "Hsi-Lai," which means "coming to the West." It is specifically devoted to nurturing Buddhist missionaries and propagating the teachings of the Buddha in Western society. By 2010, Buddhists in North America numbered about 3.6 million. As with Islam, the spread of Buddhism in the West owes a lot to the localization of the faith, as the increasing numbers of non-Asians converts to Buddhism apply its spirituality and doctrine to Western concerns and values.[41]

---

[39] Ibid.

[40] See Dan Smyer Yü, "Buddhist Conversion in the Contemporary World," in *The Oxford Handbook of Religious Conversion*, ed. Rambo and Farhadian, 465–87. The Taiwanese Venerable Master Xuanhua (1918–1995) epitomized the missionary consciousness. His effort led, among other things, to the building of one of the largest Buddhist temples in North America.

[41] Western Buddhism, for instance, is "lay-oriented rather than monastic-centered" and far more oriented towards social and environmental activism. Ibid., 475–78.

The Christian Experience

Possibly no other world faith exemplifies these worldwide trans-formations linked to migration more acutely than Christianity.[42] Christianity's rate of expansion over the last one hundred years ex-ceeds any other period in its two thousand-year history. Signifi-cantly, the vast majority of this recent growth, in terms of adherents and churches, has taken place in areas of the globe in which Chris-tian presence was statistically insignificant at the beginning of the previous century.[43] Not only are Christians now present in each of the world's 239 countries but the phenomenal expansion of the faith outside previous heartlands also represents "the greatest ever pro-liferation of converted cultures and consequently of Christian life-styles."[44] Equally noteworthy, Christians are the most evenly dispersed on the planet of any major religious group. According to 2010 estimates, "roughly equal numbers of Christians" live in Eu-rope (26 percent), Latin America and the Caribbean (24 percent) and sub-Saharan Africa (24 percent).[45]

This finding confirms one of the most momentous religious transformations of our time: namely, the re-emergence of Christian-ity as a non-Western religion. In 1900, less than one-fifth (18 percent) of the world's Christians resided outside Europe or North America. By 2000, more than 60 percent of all Christians resided outside the West, and Christianity continues to decline in its previous heart-lands at a dramatic rate. The 26 percent of Christians now living in

---

[42] See Todd M. Johnson and Kenneth R. Ross, eds., *Atlas of Global Christianity, 1910–2010* (Edinburgh: Edinburgh University Press, 2009), 8-9; *Global Religious Diversity: Half of the Most Religiously Diverse Countries are in Asia-Pacific Region*, Pew Research Center (2014); *The Global Religious Landscape: A Report on the Size and Distribution of the World's Major Religious Groups as of 2010*; Wesley Granberg-Michaelson, *From Times Square to Timbuktu: The Post-Christian West meets the Non-Western Church* (Grand Rapids: Wm. B. Eerdmans, 2013), 7–27.

[43] "World Christianity, 1910–2010," *International Bulletin of Missionary Research* 34, no. 1 (January, 2010): 32.

[44] Andrew F. Walls, "Scholarship, Mission and Globalisation: Some Reflections on the Christian Scholarly Vocation in Africa," *Journal of African Christian Thought* 9, no. 2 (December, 2006): 35.

[45] *The Global Religious Landscape: A Report on the Size and Distribution of the World's Major Religious Groups as of 2010*, 10.

Europe reflects a massive decline from 66 percent in 1910. In 1900, over 71 percent of the world's evangelicals (admittedly a rather fluid category) lived in just two countries—the United States and the United Kingdom.[46] By 2010, 75 percent of evangelicals lived outside the West.[47] If current trends continue, Africa and Latin America will together account for half the Christians in the world by 2025. Tremendous gains in Asia, where Christianity is reportedly growing at twice the rate of the overall population (though it only accounted for 8.2 percent of the overall population in 2010) is also part of the new picture.[48] Such is the upsurge in conversions to Christianity in China that some speculate that more Christians may be attending worship in that country (not counting the substantial Chinese Christian diaspora) than in the United States.[49]

This historic shift in global Christianity's demographic center of gravity has profound implications for virtually every major segment of the world Christian movement, whether Protestant or Roman Catholic. At least half of all Anglicans and more than a third of Mennonites are African; while Latin America accounts for some 40 percent of all Roman Catholics worldwide.[50] Even Mormonism—a faith that remains decidedly American in its governance, image, and orientation, and only recently accepted blacks to the priesthood—is marked by these trends. In 1996, Mormons living in the United States became a minority within the LDS Church for the first time; and, with increasing gains in Africa, the Caribbean, and South America, Mormonism is becoming decreasingly white or

---

[46] See Patrick J. Johnstone, *The Future of the Global Church: History, Trends and Possibilities* (Colorado Springs: Biblica, 2011), 145.

[47] Granberg-Michaelson, *From Times Square to Timbuktu*, 10. A century earlier, in 1910, Europe and North America had accounted for some 90 percent of the total.

[48] *Christianity in its Global Context, 1970–2020*, 7.

[49] For more on this and the rise of Christianity in Asia, see Granberg-Michaelson, *From Times Square to Timbuktu*, 8–9. Patrick Johnstone also estimates that the evangelical population in China "will probably have far surpassed that of the U.S. by 2050." Johnstone, *The Future of the Global Church*, 145.

[50] Less well known is the fact that in the twentieth century Africa registered the fastest growth of Catholicism of any continent since the beginning of Christianity. See John L. Allen, "Global South will Shape the Future Catholic Church," *National Catholic Reporter* (October 7, 2005).

Anglo-Saxon and increasingly brown and black in its demographic profile.

All this is to say that twenty-first century Christianity is predominantly non-white; and, by 2050, perhaps only about one-fifth of the world's Christians will be white Caucasian. Today, more Christians worldwide speak Spanish than any than any other language; and this by a wide margin.[51] Inevitably, the new global Christianity is also marked by an immense diversity of expressions, theological understanding, forms of worship, spiritual dynamism, biblical interpretation, and responses to critical issues of the day. These developments raise important questions about ecclesial identity, theological priorities, and power differentials within global Christian movements. "As Roman Catholicism in the future speaks with an African and Hispanic accent," comments one observer, "it will also speak in tongues."[52] The globalization of many Christian denominations means that tensions between diversity and distinctiveness must be constantly negotiated and the gap between representativeness and controlling authority constructively attended.

In the American context where notions of global preeminence remain entrenched, these transformations are particularly unsettling. But the fact remains that constituencies in the non-Western world will play an increasing role in setting the global agenda within twenty-first century Christianity. And global migratory flows augment these trends.

Christian Migrants

Recent data indicates that Christians constitute nearly half (49 percent) of this international migrant movement.[53] In Europe and America (the two top destinations of international migrants), the high proportion of Christians among the world's international migrants is

---

[51] Todd M. Johnson and Sun Young Chung, "Christianity's Center of Gravity, AD 33–2100," in *Atlas of Global Christianity 1910–2010*, ed. Todd M. Johnson and Kenneth R. Ross (Edinburgh: Edinburgh University Press, 2009), 51.

[52] Allen, "Global South will Shape the Future Catholic Church," 20.

[53] Phillip Connor and Catherine Tucker, "Religion and Migration around the Globe: Introducing the Global Religion and Migration Database,"

conspicuously absent from the heated immigration debates. In both contexts, the public discourse on immigration focuses almost exclusively on Muslim immigrants and illegal immigration, respectively. It is little known that 43 percent of the immigrants to the European Union are Christian—compared to 30 percent who are Muslim.[54] For European Christianity, the new wave of immigrants has brought both diversity and vitality. In the case of the United States, some 70 percent of these new immigrants are estimated to be Christian; the highest proportion of any developed country.[55] To put it in crude numerical terms, as many as 35 million Christians have potentially been added to the American population in the last few decades. While this may go some way to counter significant decline (especially within the Roman Catholic faith), it has already fostered a "de-Europeanizing" of American Christianity[56]—a trend that will

---

International Migration Review 45, no. 4 (2011): 994. Muslims constitute the second largest religious group of migrants (27 percent). This finding is consistent with the fact that a good proportion of international migrants now come from the new heartlands of Christianity in the non-Western world

[54] *Faith on the Move: The Religious Affiliation of International Migrants* (Pew Research Center, 2012), 54. See also, Joanne Appleton, "Beyond the Stereotypes: The Realities of Migration in Europe Today," *Vista* 10 (2012). When the entire foreign-born population is counted (regardless of origin) the percentage of Christians is much higher: 56 percent of all immigrants in the EU identify themselves as Christian; more than twice the number who say they are Muslim (27 percent). An earlier (2003) study found that almost half (48.5 percent) of the estimated 24 million migrants in the EU were Christian or "belonged to Christian churches." Darrell Jackson and Alessia Passarelli, *Mapping Migration: Mapping Churches' Response* (Brussels: World Council of Churches, 2008), 29.

[55] Connor and Tucker, "Religion and Migration around the Globe: Introducing the Global Religion and Migration Database," 11f. See also *The Religious Affiliation of U.S. Immigrants: Majority Christian, Rising Share of Other Faiths.*

[56] Cf. Fenggang Yang and Helen Ebaugh, "Transformations in New Immigrant Religions and their Global Implications," *American Sociological Review* 66, no. 2 (April, 2001): 271; also, R. Stephen Warner, "Coming to America," *The Christian Century* (February 10, 2004): 23; and Ebaugh and Chafetz, *Religion and the New Immigrants*, 14.

accelerate as the non-white segment of the American population continues to rise.[57]

Global Pluralism, the Church and Theological Education

The violent face of global pluralism—exemplified by genocidal conflicts, ferocious acts of violence linked to extremist ideologies, and escalating levels of social hostility around the world—is beyond the purview of this presentation. It must be said, however, that the commonplace term "religious violence" betrays a secular understanding in which religion is a strand of social existence distinct from politics, economics, culture, and so on. Thus, attributing specific acts of violence to religion not only channels mistrust of religion, it also implies a view of the latter as a private or discreet pursuit disconnected from other human undertakings. Not only is this understanding distinctively Western, and recently so, it is also incompatible with the worldview of the vast majority of societies and cultures for whom "religion" encompasses all of life (the cultural, political, and social, etc.) and is not limited to matters of faith and piety. For societies or communities in which religious adherence signifies a way of life, religiosity that neglects social need or ignores economic oppression is an inherent contradiction. As Scott Thomas puts it, "faith informs the daily struggles of millions in confronting larger political conflicts regarding democracy, human rights, and economic development."[58] The problem with the "religious violence" label is not that the activity it describes is free from religious dogma but rather that it tends to obscure the wider realities that stimulate extreme hostility.[59]

Acts of violence unleashed by groups that claim religious identity or ideology have been invariably induced by broader experiences and historical developments. The same processes of

---

[57] For more on this, see Jehu J. Hanciles, *Beyond Christendom: Globalization, African Migration, and the Transformation of the West* (Maryknoll, NY: Orbis Books, 2008), 229–49, 276–302; and Granberg-Michaelson, *From Times Square to Timbuktu*, 79–95.

[58] Thomas, "A Globalized God," 101.

[59] For a helpful treatment, see Karen Armstrong, *Fields of Blood: Religion and the History of Violence* (Toronto: Knopf Canada, 2014); also, "The Roots of Jihadism: A Struggle that Shames," *The Economist* (January 17, 2015).

globalization that enable structures of domination and exploitation also extend the reach and impact of sectarian hatred and strife, not least by granting masses of disaffected youth (alienated by deep social divisions and cultural rejection) access to vitriolic ideas that find expression in religious tenets. This is not to excuse or rationalize barbaric acts of terrorism that claim even more victims among fellow believers and must be confronted. But it also invites a recognition that what is viewed as insulting to a religious faith is often experienced as a hateful attack on a society or way of life. Worse still, aggressive secularism—which deems its particular principles to be universal, regards alternative belief systems as unacceptable heresies, and is often tied to national ideals or championed by the state—looks suspiciously like a religious system with a history of bloody violence of its own.

The "kingdom of God" concept stands in stark contrast to these failures of human society that are generally fomented in cultural difference and unequal power. It evokes God's presence and saving power in the world and expresses the good news of salvation for the poor and oppressed. Its "preferential option for the poor," celebrated in liberation theology, is not an exclusivist proposition. In one sense, all are poor, deprived of full humanity by the tyranny of sin. But the focus on the poor and victims of oppression (including religious oppression) reflects the simple truth that the sick are usually most conscious of their need for a physician (Luke 5:31). It is not necessary to explore the variety of interpretations of this powerful concept to confirm that it combines both proclamation and demonstration and that it found its fullest manifestation in the life and ministry of Jesus.

For our purposes, it is crucial to note that, in terms of its purview and purpose, the kingdom of God gives powerful expression to the global pluralism sanctioned in the Babel story. The long-awaited Messiah announced to the Jews appears among a stateless and oppressed people; his public activities are largely confined to a context (Galilee) with a sizeable Gentile population; his ministry cuts across social, ethnic, and economic divides, eschewing the exclusive claims of any particular social group. The pluralist intent of his message is superbly captured in the declaration that "the kingdom of heaven is like a net that . . . caught fish of every kind" (Matt 13:47).

Throughout the centuries to the present day, the pluralistic and universal mandate of the kingdom of God motif has repeatedly and relentlessly exploded the parochial cities of Babel erected by the church in every age. Such efforts, present throughout the world even today, seek to imprison the revelation of Christ within a particular race, nation, culture, ethnicity, even language. But the kingdom of God revealed in Christ unceasingly calls the church to affirm and celebrate that glorious vision of the end of the age depicted in Revelation 7:9, "a great multitude that no one could count, from every nation, from all tribes and peoples and languages, standing before the throne and before the Lamb."

For both the church and the theological academy, these insights have particular relevance in a new age of globalization marked by extraordinary migrations, unprecedented interpenetration among the world's peoples and cultures, and historic transformations within world Christianity. There is space here only to highlight a few cogent elements of this new reality and the challenges they present in the Western/American context.

The American Church

It goes without saying that the rapid, unprecedented cultural shift underway in American society as a result of immigration has major implications for American denominations. The most dynamic and fastest growing churches in the United States today are either linked to immigrant communities (which tend to be self-consciously evangelistic) or incorporate a wide range of racial and cultural groups in their structures. In the 16 million-member Southern Baptist Convention (SBC), for instance, ethnic minority membership grew from 4 percent in 1990 to 20 percent in 2008.[60] Of the 1,458 SBC congregations planted in 2007, half were nonwhite (i.e., formed by African Americans and other ethnicities). The SBC currently claims 3,200 Hispanic churches—with a stated goal of 7,000 by 2020.[61] Former SBC President Paige Patterson pointedly declared that "the future of the Southern Baptist Convention has to be a multiracial,

---

[60] Matthew Soerens and Jenny Hwang, *Welcoming the Stranger: Justice, Compassion & Truth in the Immigration Debate* (Downers Grove, IL: IVP Books, 2009), Kindle Locations 1797–1800.

[61] Elizabeth Dias, "Evangélicos!," *Time* (April 15, 2013): 23.

multiethnic future, or quite frankly, it has no future."[62] In similar vein, Lovett H. Weems Jr. of The United Methodist Church (UMC)—a church whose US membership is over 90 percent white—asserts that "there is no future for The United Methodist Church in the US unless it can demonstrate that it can reach more people, younger people and more diverse people."[63]

Hardly any denomination in America can claim exemption to this prognosis. This makes all the more astounding the reality that, among Protestant groups, relations between the new immigrant churches and homegrown churches or denominations are marked (with few exceptions) by disengagement and alienation. This lack of sustained interaction or meaningful association is rooted in paternalism, cultural rejection, a widespread tendency to view nonwhite immigration as a problem, and persistent notions of the non-Western world as the "mission field." Most of all, it reflects spiritual dissonance and divergences in theological outlook and reveals long-standing tensions within the worldwide church.[64] Massive immigration has brought Christians from diverse communities throughout the world into closer proximity than ever before with unprecedented opportunities for mutual engagement and intercultural partnership in the work of God's kingdom. Often "Babel" wins out! But our common commitment to the kingdom of God daily calls us to a new understanding and fresh perspectives.

Clearly, forging new relationships or interactions marked by constructive engagement and meaningful cooperation (between immigrant Christian groups and homegrown Christian communities) requires radical adjustments on both sides: including determined efforts to overcome the legacy of inequitable global power structures and a preparedness to think differently about the mission of the church in an era when no single center or nation can claim preeminence. This must be anchored by a shared commitment to the work of the kingdom. As Andrew Walls attests, in some areas of the West immigrant Christians increasingly "provide the first contact with

---

[62] Soerens and Hwang, *Welcoming the Stranger*, KL 1799–1800.

[63] Barbara Dunlap-Berg, "UMC Membership Reaches 12 Million Worldwide," *Church Exclusive* (2012).

[64] I offer more on this elsewhere. See Jehu J. Hanciles, "Migrants as Missionaries, Missionaries as Outsiders: Reflections on African Christian Presence in Western Societies," *Mission Studies* 30, no. 1 (2013): 64–85.

Christianity as a living faith" for many within the indigenous Western population "who are untouched by traditional cultural Christianity."[65] To be sure, immigrant Christian communities must contend with intergenerational tensions and social marginalization. But, beyond providing new spiritual vitality and helping to nurture the next generation of Western Christians, they also have a role to play in bridging the divide afflicting some global Christian communities over major doctrinal and social issues.

It is also worth noting that the new Christian immigrants come from contexts of religious plurality and, as such, have a lot to offer an American church that is confronted with a diversity of faiths for the first time. The encounter between Christianity and other world religions in the American context has yet to fully engage public consciousness, but Christian immigrants who come from a variety of multi-faith societies represent a vital resource if the church is to play a meaningful role in the coming debate. It is worth noting, for instance, that immigrants from contexts where Christianity is a minority faith tend to have a different perspective on issues such as "religious dialogue." In the Western situation "religious dialogue" is typically initiated by adherents of the majority faith as a specific exercise in which the different sides participate. Asian Christians, however, "live permanently amid the practitioners of these great religions." For them, observes American-Asian scholar Jonathan Tan, dialogue cannot be reduced to an occasional event or planned encounter; it is "a daily dialogue of life witness with . . . fellow Asian neighbors who are followers of the great religious traditions of Asia."[66]

The Theological Academy

The reshaping of global Christianity has huge implications for Western theological education, including the need to incorporate global perspectives and fully account for new realities that require

---

[65] Andrew F. Walls, "Migration and Evangelization: The Gospel and Movement of Peoples in Modern Times," *The Covenant Quarterly* 63, no. 1 (February, 2005): 22.

[66] Jonathan Y. Tan, "Rethinking the Relationship between Christianity and World Religions, and Exploring Its implications for Doing Christian Mission in Asia," *Missiology* 39, no. 4 (October, 2011): 501.

new models or conceptual tools. This remains a daunting task for most theological programs, made more so by the near hegemonic dominance of Western intellectual traditions and academic production. Given recent transformations within Christianity, the need for attentiveness to non-Western models and perspectives has never been greater, but the structures of economic globalization and a history of Western intellectual hegemony stand firmly in the way. How this is so invites brief comment.

The last couple of decades have witnessed the lively growth of non-Western academic production and publications in all major theological disciplines. Since the 1980s, new degree-granting institutions have proliferated in Africa, Latin America, and South Korea.[67] But many, if not most, maintain syllabi that follow the Western model. In some cases, this is due to accreditation requirements that remain tied to European models and prescriptions. In other cases, dependence on Western donors and support to a great extent shapes programs and library resources. When combined with the forces of economic globalization, this also means that "theological research and publications from Europe are present in African theological libraries, where theological research from Africa is to a great extent absent."[68]

Similarly, there is ample evidence of the rapidly growing contribution of non-Western scholars in terms of academic production and collaborations in research and writing in all major theological disciplines. But far too many reveal an outlook that remains captive to Western training and intellectual traditions, in some measure because they depend on Western-based publishers for sale and distribution of their ideas. The following comment by the editors of the recently published *Global Dictionary of Theology* illustrates the point:

> It was . . . surprising the number of scholars from the Global South who tended to do theology in the manner of their Northern teachers . . . [that] entries drafted by theologians from Asia, Africa, and Latin America did not differ significantly

[67] Cf. Joel Carpenter, "New Evangelical Universities: Cogs in World System, or Players in a New Game," *International Journal of Frontier Missions* 20, no. 2 (Summer, 2003): 55–65.

[68] Dietrich Werner, "Theological Education in the Changing Context of World Christianity—An Unfinished Agenda," *International Bulletin of Missionary Research* 35, no. 2 (April 2011): 96.

THE VOCATION OF THEOLOGY

from entries that would have been written by their European or North American counterparts.[69]

Whether or not increasing access to internet resources or online databases—still beyond the reach of most institutions and programs—will make a difference to this culture of intellectual passivity and dependence is difficult to say. Meanwhile, as Dietrich Werner suggests, Western dominance of online educational systems has resulted in "an increased tendency to create programs affiliated with American or other Western theological colleges that operate as branches in countries of the South."[70]

The Role of the Western Theological Curriculum

The claim that Western intellectual hegemony remains one of the most enduring challenges for theological education in the non-Western world is perhaps overused, but it cannot be dismissed. Not many will dispute Joel Carpenter's observation that "the ideas and research of Asians and Africans are still treated mainly as the exotic raw materials with which the Northern intellectual aristocrats can furnish their ivory towers"; and that while "Northerners continue to assume the right to intellectual rule . . . Southern intellectual development remains stunted."[71] Yet, it is foolhardy to think that non-Western theological scholarship and training can be wholly undertaken in local or regional isolation.

In a new age of globalization, the thickening and multifarious strands that link educational systems and academic production around the world are an unavidable reality. The United States still

---

[69] William A. Dyrness and Veli-Matti Karkkainen, eds., *Global Dictionary of Theology: A Resource for the Worldwide Church* (Downers Grove, IL: IVP Academic, 2008), xi.

[70] Werner, "Theological Education in the Changing Context of World Christianity—An Unfinished Agenda," 96.

[71] Joel Carpenter, "The Christian Scholar in an Age of World Christianity," in *Christianity and the Soul of the University: Faith as a Foundation for Intellectual Community*, ed. Douglas V. Henry and Michael D. Beaty (Grand Rapids: Baker Academic, 2006), 81.

receives some 21 percent of the world's foreign students.[72] The Association of Theological Schools (a North American body) reports that foreign students accounted for 10 percent of the student population in ATS schools in 2012. Thus, while the growing interconnections between the West and the non-West in terms of theological education may include elements of hegemonic exploitation, these same interconnections and the web of relationships that come with them are also indispensable for the development of theological education in the non-Western world. As Carpenter observes, what the academic inequities in question call for are new efforts at building "just and reconciling relationships."

Western institutions are trying, and most are trying very hard, to pursue "internationalization" and to emphasize the tremendous gains of diversity. Unfortunately, these objectives commonly reflect economic calculation or ideological commitment to righting past wrongs rather than vested interest in the transformations that genuine internationalization would entail for programs and curricula. Within theological institutions, in fact, it is not uncommon for recognition (even celebration) of the new shape of world Christianity to coexist with obliviousness of its profound implications for theological education, or insufficient awareness that exclusive dependence on Western voices, models, and constructs significantly blunts our capacity to ask the right questions, to understand new realities, or tell the whole story.[73]

Our consciousness and experience of being a global community of faith is greater than ever before; but a fundamental reorientation

[72] In the 2012–13 academic year the United States "hosted a record 819,644 international students." Neil G. Ruiz, *The Geography of Foreign Students in U.S. Higher Education: Origins and Destinations* (Washington, DC: Brookings Institute, 2014), 1.

[73] Andrew Walls' examination of the specific implications for church (or Christian) history makes for compelling reading. See Andrew F. Walls, "Eusebius Tries Again: Reconceiving the Study of Christian History," *International Bulletin of Missionary Research* 24, no. 3 (July, 2000): 105–111. For my own modest contributions, see Jehu J. Hanciles, "New Wine in Old Wine- skins: Critical Reflections on Writing and Teaching a Global Christian History," *Missiology: An International Review* 35, no. 3 (July, 2006): 361–82; and "The Future of Missiology as a Discipline: A View from the Non-Western World," *Missiology: An International Review* 42, no. 2 (April, 2014): 121–38.

is needed for programs (or courses) to truly engage or incorporate global perspectives and experiences as part of an overall effort to provide the best training for a new generation of leaders. Leading theological institutions like Candler need to address this need as a matter of priority and academic integrity, being careful to distinguish between strategic and symbolic action. Our school is certainly moving in the right direction. Between 1992 and 2012, the number of "students of color" entering our school rose from 7 percent to 32 percent, and the number of international students in all programs increased from 4 percent to 10 percent. Over the last three years we have vigorously pursued a multifaceted "internationalization program," and the creation of a new multifaith position signals clear commitment to theological education that trains students to think seriously about dominant issues of our day.

But there is so much more to be done as we pursue a vision of serving the worldwide church in a new age of global pluralism. Unless it leads to transformations within institutional life and impacts the quality of our programs, internationalization may amount to little more than a promotional asset. Among other things, this calls for time-consuming investment in relationships, painstaking collaborations, and adaptive structures. Cultivating cultural diversity within our student body, faculty and staff ought to reflect our determination to be a certain kind of community and a willingness to call our denominations to a new kind of existence. But while it is challenging enough to attract and maintain diverse representation within our programs—especially regarding the presence of qualified students of the non-Western world—we must also be vigilant about overcoming the common deception of pursuing representation without making room for those voices. This calls for a willingness to evaluate existing curricula with a view to promoting the development of academic programs and courses that inculcate global perspectives, based on candid acknowledgement that no segment of humanity has all the insights and no particular heritage can tell the full story.

Any one of these objectives represents a significant long-term challenge. Taken together they amount to a formidable undertaking. The way forward may be daunting, but the need is no less compelling. Navigating the new and exciting frontiers of the world Christian movement calls for multiple lenses and critical embrace of a multiplicity of voices and experiences. If foresight is indeed "the secret ingredient of success," then inspiration for the task at hand is derived in part from the prophetic vision of "a great multitude that no one could count, from every nation, from all tribes and peoples and languages, standing before the throne and before the Lamb" (Rev 7:9). Until that great day, our commitment to the kingdom of God requires unwavering determination to affirm and to cultivate "fish of every kind."

CHAPTER 13

On-the-Job Courage

Teresa L. Fry Brown

Centennial Academic Conference Sermon
March 20, 2014
Text: 2 Samuel 23:20

"If it had not been for the Lord on our side, where would we be?"
(cf. Ps 124:1). "I have been young, and am now old, but I have
never seen the righteous forsaken, nor God's seed begging for
bread" (cf. Ps 37:25). As the old hymn says, "When I think of the
goodness of Jesus / And all he keeps doing for me / My soul cries out,
Hallelujah! / I thank the Lord for saving me."

The invitation to preach the closing sermon of this conference
has driven me to distraction all week. Looking over Candler's vision
statement, I noted that it is packed with action: "continually
strengthen, internationally distinguished, intentionally diverse,
committed to educating, expanding knowledge, deepening spiritual life, strengthening the public witness, building upon the
breadth of Christian traditions, positive transformation of the
Church and the world." And as I contemplated this preaching moment, I understood that Candler is much more than words on a
website and provocative conversations and productive research and
scholarship. Candler also represents an active engagement in doing
more than what we talk about; we actually have to get up off our
seats of do-nothingness and do something.

One needs only to look with even a superficial analysis of the
current social, political, cultural, and spiritual landscape to understand that we are in need of intellectual activism. Surrounded by
perpetual racial and gender microaggressions toward the "Other,"
commodification of faith, and so-called "Prosperity Gospel"
advocates asking for $65 million for a private jet while their

congregants cannot afford to ride MARTA. A cult of celebrity and sanctified selfishness; cyber spirituality and decaying ministries; vapid exclusionary theologies and doctrines and laws; blurred lines between fantasy, entertainment and reality; mass killings, hate crimes and brutality based on social constructs of race and gender religiosity interpretations; state sanctioned lynching; as the physical and spiritual body count exponentially growing. At times it seems we're surrounded by the walking dead, weighed down with the world standards of success and happiness and status and bank account balances and wearable wealth. Caught in a DuBoisian spiritual double consciousness, striving to become someone else, competing for crumbs and not recognizing that we are who we are as others looked at us with amused contempt.

I would like to call your attention to one passage of scripture that was given to me last night—2 Samuel 23:20:

> Benaiah son of Jehoiada was a valiant warrior from Kabzeel, a doer of great deeds; he struck down two sons of Ariel of Moab. He also went down and killed a lion in a pit on a day when the snow had fallen.

The topic I will attend to for our brief time together is "On-the-Job Courage." On-the-job courage is a state of quality of mind that enables one to face danger, fear, with self-possession and confidence and resolution. In this particular passage, David has a "my soul looks back and wonder how I got over" kind of moment. And in a divine oracle, he begins to reflect on his life and realizes that he did not succeed without the help of others. David received the praise, but God surrounded with people, understudies, background singers, support systems, ministering angels, wise counsel, administrative staff, colleagues, bodyguards, armor bearers that contributed to his strength and his ability. He was supported and ministered and protected and nurtured and counseled and saved by a group in the text of mighty men of God. A ragtag army that had lived in the wilderness, and they followed all of his orders and went wherever David went. Through victory and defeat, through war and peace, through prosperity and famine, their blood and sweat and isolation and pain and suffering and tears and joy and love all made Candler what it was suppose to be. They understood David's assignment was from God, they suffered when David suffered, they took care of

David, they guarded his life and risked their lives for David, they learned to face danger and fear with self-possession and confidence—with courage to do their jobs.

There is no record that any of them tried to be like David or write like David or dress like David or sing like David or dance like David or hijack David's credentials or plot to take David's throne or blog his personal life or sell their inheritance for instant gratification or spend more time working on mess than the message or ran away when the things got rough. In David's remembrances of these men stood out. One of them, much younger than David was exemplary in a aspects of his job performance. One of the thirty, Benaih ("made by God") provides a metaphor for what we need to do to activate all the things we have heard these days that we have been together.

Second Samuel 23:20b: "He also went down and killed a lion in a pit on a day when snow had fallen." "He," Benaiah; "also," that means he had done other things and we do not know anything about his life other than his father's name. But he pledges allegiance to this king. He was a courageous warrior, David's bodyguard, chief of his mercenary corps; he was later promoted to be the general of Solomon's guard, and held the greatest respect among the Thirty. In one account he went to battle with a small club, took a spear out of a giant's hand and killed him. David evidently was captivated by Beniah's courage.

The text indicates "He also went down"—like a call—individual, corporate, gradual, nurtured or cataclysimic. We don't know any information about why he went down like the call that God gives us and we do not have a clue why God is calling us but we got to go anyway. And we don't know how he arrived at the site, if he was alone, or if he had properly prepared for the situation. Like when God sends you some place and does not tell you how you going to get there, if you are going to have any money when you get there, if the people are going to want to hear you when you get there, if everybody is going to get up and walk out because you weren't the last person that preached.

All we know is that he went down. He also went down and killed a lion. Lions are mentioned 135 times in the Old Testament and are known for their strength. Asiatic lions, young swift lions were herbivores, they ate plants but old lions with their teeth and strength failing were carnivores, they ate human beings like that front row in your churches. Just saying, just saying. We are not told why the lion was killed. Sometimes peope, places and things are removed from our path and no one but God knows how or why. We are not told if Beniah was wounded in the encounter. Some of our wounds, problems, issues, habits, and needs are hidden from others. On this journey, just like Benaiah, we will have to face our lions. Hadn't David said, "I find myself in a pride of lions who are wild for a taste of human flesh; their teeth are lances and arrows; their tongues are sharp daggers"(cf. Ps 57:4)?

We will have to face our lions. Lions that are sent to seek and kill and destroy; lions whose mouths are ready to critique our response to doing God's will; lions who look at the work we are doing and become jealous but they're too lazy to do it themselves; lions that can't wait to tear us down. Lions that accuse us of worshiping other gods, lions who want to change, charge us with something unsaved or atheist, like students do their first year when they hear their professors teach. And lions that say we do not pray enough and lions that whisper lies and then smile in our faces but plot to bring us down. Lions that rather gossip than talk with us, lions whose appointment and anointing is to stay on our cases so that we will pray more. Lions who skip class and want to copy off of our paper, but critique how we said it in the first place, old and tired, feeble and limping, and out of breath lions that can't do the work but want to stop our work. Lions are everywhere. In the struggle to follow God's commandments, in the effort to keep God's commandments, in the faces of people who still refuse to honor God's creative force—lions, lions, lions. We may be wounded in the house of our friends and disappointment seems to be in the very air we breath.

But God always has a plan for us. God has already given us everything we need to take care of whatever assignment God has given us, to confront those challenges in the next century. He also went down and killed a lion in a pit. A pit is that large natural artificial cavity, an abyss, a hole in the ground, a depression like a low point in our ministry when we think we are doing God's work and no matter how hard we try nothing seems to work out. We find ourselves in a pit where there are times of disappointment, nobody comes to our meetings, and nobody seems to remember our purpose, and people don't take our classes because we don't look like them and we're so tired that we don't think about getting up again. Then grief begins to grip our hearts and we don't know what to do, we're sad, there's tears, there's fears, there's confusion, there's disappointment. At times we think we will lose our mind and even our family abandons us. When we find ourselves in the pit we have options. We can quit, lie, fight, adapt change, or and move to another pit. We can lie and pretend that everything is okay. We can fight each other. We can adapt and do what other people tell us to do, we can change and let God work through us, or we can die on the job.

"He also went down and killed a lion in a pit on a day that snow had fallen." Snow, the hexagonal lattice ice crystals that are common in Palestine in the hills in the wintertime. Sometimes two feet and sometimes just a little on the ground. He was in a snow-covered pit like the first few years of our faith journey when we discover that our ministerial parents and the elders in the church and our Sunday school teachers and our seminary professors and our trusted advisors couldn't teach us anything at all. The rest of the journey is like a snowy day, sometimes beautiful and it's tranquil, but we start moving and it becomes difficult sometimes to navigate where God tells us to go. We slip and we slide and sometimes we crawl and fall and we have good traction and move forward and sometimes we have to advance and retreat.

Can you imagine Benaiah standing there wondering where all the people were that said they would be there when he started out? Where are his boys and his girls, and BFFs, and his ride and die crew, and his social network and his faculty colleagues, and those who said they would be there? But are now stabbing him in the back, it seems, because he is all by himself. Can you see him strategizing? After the conference is over and you have received all this wonderful information do you just put it on the shelf until the next conference? Or you take all the information that you supposedly gleaned and start to put it into action? You know, what do you do with all that.

Can you see him? Over four hundred thousand apps and he could not find anything about defeating the lion. No matter how many texts he checked out of Pitts, nothing gave him what he wanted. He tried to Google God, but that didn't work. He goes to news media but they are no help. FOX gave trumped up partisan steps, and PBS was having a pledge drive and MSNBC was recapping his earlier actions and CSPAN kept repeating the same things over and over and over again. But he didn't give up. He didn't turn away from challenging a system that seems like it was going to consume him. He didn't avoid the hard questions. He didn't become discouraged because he was the only one who believed in the cause. Maybe he remembered something from his childhood about standing up against one's enemy, maybe he reflected on what God had done for him before. All he knew was he was a warrior and had a lion in front of him. Maybe he remembered the signs that say we have to go ahead and do something. The excitement, the anticipation, looking at what you already have in front of you, listening to the voice from within, uncomfortable with what is going on but knowing you have to do something. As Gandhi reportedly said, "You may never know the results of your action but if you do nothing there will be no result."

He went down, he killed a lion in a pit on a day that snow had fallen. Perhaps miscalculating his fold but regrouping, perhaps circling or going in a straight line. Perhaps staying there for days, perhaps he had to get away so he could think about what he needed to do. Yet he killed the lion with the tools of his trade, his own experience, his own intellect, his own weapons, his own spirit, his own love, his own tools, his own resources. What happened on that day, we don't know, but the report came back that he killed the lion and left the pit. He had courage in that instance, courage to understand the power and presence and purpose and promise of God. It's not about people, places and things but about what God puts inside of us in the first place.

Now we understand on this journey of activism that there will be many nights when fear will grip us in its cold hands. We will fear failure, and fear loss, and fear humiliation and critique and alienation and even ourselves. Some of us fear success. But we serve a God who promises never to leave us or forsake us whether we are in a pit or on the mountaintop. God always asks us to do things that are not easy. But God says, "I am there with you anyway." God asks us to get on boats during storms with a whole bunch of animals. God asks us to enter fiery furnaces without protective gear. God asks us to fight giants with slingshots and pebbles, to eat out take-out meals served by a bunch of ravenous birds. God asks us to sleep while lions are all around us and we will get up without a hair on us at all. God asks us to share a grain of food with strangers and to give half of our coveted designer wardrobe to someone whose is naked and to pray with someone we can't even see.

On-the-job courage insists that we remember if God is for us, nobody can be against us. If God who created all things and promised never to leave us, if God who continually supports us and feeds us, if God is before us who can be against us? Who is big and bad enough to get God out of the way? Who can destroy what God has already planted inside of us? Who can reverse anything God already has planned for us? Oh, they will try, but the God I serve is too bad for words. With God on our side how can we possibly lose? God who has rescued us from death before can do it again. Those of us who have entered pits, once or twice or thirty or forty times or find ourselves in pits every day, we have to still continue to develop a courage to move out of our comfort zones, to end the ad nauseam discussions and get to work. To use our intellectual activism to think through what we need to do and engage questions of faith and stop just talking about things, to identify evil and engage it, to take responsibility for our own complicity in silence about things around us.

God will empower us, protect and direct us. Along the spines of our fear and our frustration, around the edges of our despair and depression, over the precipice of loneliness and lovelessness, through the valley of death and darkness, across the deserts of separation and sadness, under the weight of discrimination and denigration, above the winds of apathy and adversity.

My friends in this sanctuary, as we close this conference, I hope we all learned something, that there is much work to do. But not one person can do it alone. We each however have to go down into our God-designated pits and kill our own lions on snowy days like Benaiah. We don't need another news conference. God knows we don't. We don't need another business meeting. We don't need another media talking head doing a postmortem analysis on what should have been done. We don't need another hashtag or another t-shirt campaign. We need to spend before the throne of God saying, "What do I need to do to make the world better." When we accept the responsibility to move from being reactive to proactive. When we give equal weight to theory and practice. When we accept that sometimes we are going to fail, but other times we are going to succeed. God is still able to keep us from falling when we are sliding. Now is the time for on-the-job courage; for learning as we go courage, for may lose some of our so-called friends courage; for God's got my back courage; for I will no longer occupy space without doing what God has called me to do courage; for "I can do all things through Christ" courage; for I serve a God who can do anything but fail courage; for I don't know about tomorrow but I know who is in charge of tomorrow courage; for I learned to look for the light when everybody else says it's dark courage; for I experience a living God in places that they tell me is already dead courage.

As we leave this place, I pray that we all will develop the kind of courage to reclaim the legacy of all persons, and ethnicities, and faiths who built the foundation of this country. To regenerate our communities, to affirm the richness of our cultures, to reconstruct our institutions of faith, the courage to act with ferocious fortitude to value different opinions, try to find new ways of reaching a conclusion, have a mind to work together and to share a cup of cold water, as my grandmother would say, "In Jesus' name." Courage to perform with indelible intentionality, to impact those who are loveless, to embrace those that are lonely, to wash those that are covered with the dirt of this world, to eliminate searing critiques of those who don't look like us or love like us or dress like us or worship like us. To proceed with a sedulous assurance to reach those that are locked out, to stand for those who have no strength, to speak for those who have no voice, to remove all the barriers of dehumanizing other people. To eliminate our own prejudices, to work to believe the report of the re-abused, to aid a sister with no hope, to walk with a brother who has been beaten down, to teach a new generation about freedom faith. To speak truth to power even if we are the power that is keeping everything bottled up. The courage to engage with vision to develop our own lives, to support service everywhere, to go where we don't think we can go, to work even when we think we are too tired to work. To mentor our replacements, to intercede for those that don't have equal access, to educate someone else, to liberate someone else, to quench the thirst of someone else, to feed the souls of someone else, to take ordinary water and make it life affirming wine, to have unmitigated gall, to have on-the-job courage, to see the invisible, to expect the incredible, to receive the impossible, to conquer anything, to have courage to reach the unreachable, and fight the unbeatable, remove the unmovable, and stand the invincible. Courage to do anything. I leave you with words of one of my social activist friends, "Wake up everybody, no more sleeping in bed, no more backward thinking, time for thinking ahead, the world has changed so very much in a hundred years from how it used to be, there is so much poverty, war, hatred, war, and poverty, but the world won't get no better, if you just let it be."[1] The world won't get no better, you got to get up, go down in the pit on a snowy day, and change the world, just you and me.

God bless you.

---

[1] Paraphrase of a portion of the lyrics of "Wake Up Everybody," originally recorded in 1975 by Harold Melvin & the Blue Notes.

173

Contributors

Teresa L. Fry Brown is Bandy Professor of Preaching, a chaired professorship created in 1986 with a gift from B. Jackson Bandy that is considered by many to be the country's premier chair in homiletics. Fry Brown has taught at Candler since 1994, and in 2010, she became the first African American woman to attain the rank of full professor. She also served as the director of Candler's Black Church Studies program until 2015. In 2012, she became the first woman to be elected as historiographer and executive director of research and scholarship of the African Methodist Episcopal Church, and in 2015, she received a Lifetime Achievement Recognition Award from the Black Religious Scholars Group of the American Academy of Religion.

Fry Brown's research interests include homiletics, womanism, womanist ethics, sociocultural transformation, and African diaspora history focusing on African American spiritual values. In addition to five monographs and four books, she has written articles and chapters for over a dozen more, including *Weary Throats and New Song: Black Women Proclaiming God's Word* (Abingdon, 2003); *Delivering the Sermon: Voice, Body and Animation in Proclamation* (Augsburg Fortress, 2008); *Can A Sistah Get a Little Help? Advice and Encouragement for Black Women in Ministry* (Pilgrim, 2008).

Jehu J. Hanciles is D. W. and Ruth Brooks Associate Professor of World Christianity. He has lived and worked in Sierra Leone, Scotland, Zimbabwe, and the United States and has been a visiting professor at schools around the world. Before coming to Candler in 2012, Hanciles was associate professor of the history of Christianity and globalization, and director of the Center for Missiological Research at Fuller Theological Seminary.

Hanciles's current research surveys the history of global Christian expansion through the lens of migration. He has written and published on a range of issues related to the history of Christianity (notably the African experience) and globalization, including two books, *Euthanasia of a Mission: African Church Autonomy in a Colonial Context* (Praeger, 2002) and *Beyond Christendom: Globalization, African Migration and the Transformation of the West* (Orbis, 2009), and countless articles. His article "The Future of Missiology as a Discipline" was one of the top ten most read articles in the field in 2015. He serves as associate editor of *Missiology*, one of the premier scholarly journals of mission studies, and on the editorial advisory committee of Studies in World Christianity (Baylor University Press).

Carl R. Holladay is Charles Howard Candler Professor of New Testament. He is also a senior fellow at the Center for the Study of Law and Religion at Emory and a popular lecturer at colleges and universities around the world. Holladay's research joins classical academic scholarship and professional application, focusing on Luke-Acts, Hellenistic Judaism (Judaism in the Greco-Roman world), and Christology. He is the author of dozens of journal articles and several books, including *A Critical Introduction to the New Testament: Interpreting the Message and Meaning of Jesus Christ* (Abingdon, 2005), which is widely used as a college ansd seminary textbook, and most recently *Acts: A Commentary*, The New Testament Library (Westminster John Knox, 2016).

With his long-time friend and colleague John H. Hayes, Holladay co-authored *Biblical Exegesis: A Beginner's Handbook* (Westminster John Knox, 1st ed., 1982; 3rd ed., 2007), a widely used introductory text on exegetical methods, theory, and practice. His four-volume series of *Fragments from Hellenistic Jewish Authors* (SBL, 1983–1996) stands as a landmark in Greco-Roman textual scholarship. In 2016–17, he served as president of the Studiorum Novi Testamenti Societas, of which he has been a member since 1979. He was elected to membertship in the American Academy of Arts and Sciences in 2017, the third Candler faculty member to be so honored.

Luke Timothy Johnson is Robert W. Woodruff Professor Emeritus of New Testament and Christian Origins. A noted scholar and award-winning teacher, Johnson taught at Yale Divinity School and Indiana University prior to arriving at Candler in 1992. His research concerns the literary, moral, and religious dimensions of the New Testament, including the Jewish and Greco-Roman contexts of early

Christianity (particularly moral discourse), Luke-Acts, the Pastoral Letters, and the Letter of James. A prolific author, he has penned thirty-one books, more than seventy scholarly articles, one hundred popular articles, and nearly two hundred book reviews.

Johnson's book *The Writings of the New Testament: An Interpretation* (Augsburg Fortress, 1st ed., 1986; 3rd ed., 2010) is widely used as a textbook in seminaries and departments of religion throughout the world. In the 1990s Johnson made national headlines with *The Real Jesus: The Misguided Quest for the Historical Jesus and the Truth of the Traditional Gospels* (HarperOne, 1996), the first book to systematically challenge the Jesus Seminar's controversial claims, among them that Jesus said only 18 percent of what the Gospels attribute to him. His book *Among the Gentiles: Greco-Roman Religion and Christianity* (Yale University Press, 2009) received the prestigious Grawemeyer Award in Religion for 2011, and *Prophetic Jesus, Prophetic Church: The Challenge of Luke-Acts to Contemporary Christians* (Eerdmans, 2011) received the Catholic Press Association Catholic Book Award in Scripture in 2012. His most recent works are *Contested Issues in Christian Origins and the New Testament: Collected Essays* (Brill, 2013) and *The Revelatory Body: Theology as Inductive Art* (Eerdmans, 2015).

Thomas G. Long is Bandy Professor Emeritus of Preaching and director of the Early Career Pastoral Leadership Program. His primary area of research is homiletics. His introductory textbook, *The Witness of Preaching* (Westminster John Knox, 1st ed., 1989; 3rd ed., 2016) has been translated into a number of languages and is widely used in theological schools around the world. In 2010, *Preaching* magazine named *The Witness of Preaching* one of the twenty-five most influential books in preaching for the last twenty-five years. Long gave the distinguished Lyman Beecher Lectures at Yale in 2006; the lectures were subsequently published in his 2009 book *Preaching from Memory to Hope* (Westminster John Knox).

Long is also deeply interested in biblical studies, practical theology, and liturgy. He has written commentaries on the biblical books of Hebrews, the Gospel of Matthew, and the Pastoral Epistles, and his books on the Christian funeral, *Accompany Them with Singing: The Christian Funeral* (Westminster John Knox, 2009) and *The Good Funeral: Death, Grief, and the Community of Care* (Westminster John

Knox, 2013; co-authored with poet and funeral director Thomas Lynch), have generated interest both in the academy and the media. His book *What Shall We Say? Evil, Suffering, and the Crisis of Faith* (Eerdmans, 2011), which addresses the issue of innocent suffering and the goodness of God, was selected as the Book of the Year for 2011, an award given by the Academy of Parish Clergy to the best book published for parish ministry in the previous year.

Ellen Ott Marshall is Associate Professor of Christian Ethics and Conflict Transformation. Prior to joining the Candler faculty in 2009, she worked with the refugee resettlement programs of Church World Service and the United Methodist Committee on Relief (UMCOR). She served as the lead writer for "God's Renewed Creation: A Call to Hope and Action," a pastoral letter and foundation document for The United Methodist Church Council of Bishops.

Marshall's current work focuses on contemporary Christian ethics, with particular attention to violence, peace-building, conflict transformation, gender and moral agency, and the dynamic relationship between faith, history, and ethics. She is the author of two books and the editor of one, and has published essays on welfare reform, the use of film to teach ethics, and the United Methodist response to war. Her book *Christians in the Public Square* (Abingdon, 2008), argues for the value of love, moral ambiguity, and theological humility in contexts of contentious debate. Her earlier book *Though the Fig Tree Does Not Blossom: Toward a Responsible Theology of Christian Hope* (Abingdon, 2006) was described as "a wonderful theological meditation on hope—a virtue so necessary for ethical commitment and change!"

Carol A. Newsom is Charles Howard Candler Professor of Old Testament and a senior fellow at Emory's Center for the Study of Law and Religion. When Newsom came to Candler in 1980, she was the second woman ever to hold a tenure-track faculty position. In 2005, she became the first female faculty member appointed to a chaired professorship at Candler. Her research focuses on the Dead Sea Scrolls, the Wisdom tradition, the book of Daniel, and apocalyptic literature. She has written and edited thirteen books and scores of articles, book chapters, translations, encyclopedia articles, and reviews.

Newsom co-edited the acclaimed *Women's Bible Commentary* (Westminster John Knox, 1st ed., 1992; 3rd ed., 2012), which explores the implications and challenges of long-held assump- tions about the Bible's portrayal of women and other marginalized groups. Her technical work with the Dead Sea Scrolls began with the publication of *Songs of the Sabbath Sacrifice: A Critical Edition* (Scholars Press, 1985) and continued through *1QHodayota with Incorporation of 1QHodayotb and 4QHodayota-f* (Clarendon Press, 2009). Her other major publications include the commentary on Job in *The New Inter- preter's Bible* (Abingdon, 1996); *The Book of Job: A Contest of Moral Imaginations* (Oxford University Press, 2003); *The Self as Symbolic Space: Constructing Identity and Community at Qumran* (Brill, 2004); and *Daniel: A Commentary* (Westminster John Knox Press, 2014). She was president of the Society of Biblical Literature in 2011, and in 2016 she became the second Candler faculty member to be inducted as a fellow of the American Academy of Arts and Sciences.

Don E. Saliers is William R. Cannon Distinguished Professor Emeritus of Theology and Worship. After retiring from the faculty in 2007, he returned to Candler in 2014 as Theologian-in-Residence. For many years he directed the Master of Sacred Music program at Emory, and was an organist and choirmaster at Cannon Chapel for thirty-five years. Before joining the Candler faculty in 1974, Saliers taught at Yale Divinity School, and has taught in summer programs at Notre Dame, Boston College, Vancouver School of Theology, St. John's University, and Boston University School of Theology.

An accomplished musician, theologian and scholar of liturgics, Saliers is the author of fifteen books on the relationship between the- ology and worship practices, as well as more than 150 articles, es- says, chapters in books and book reviews. His major works include *The Soul in Paraphrase: Prayer and the Religious Affections* (Seabury, 1980); *Worship and Spirituality* (Seabury, 1984; 2nd ed. OSL Publica- tions, 1996); *Worship as Theology: Foretaste of Glory Divine* (Abingdon, 1994); *Worship Come To Its Senses* (Abingdon, 1996); and *Music and Theology* (Abingdon, 2007). He is the coauthor of *Human Disability and the Service of God: Reassessing Religious Practice* (Abingdon, 1998) with the late Nancy Eiesland; of *The Conversation Matters: Why United Methodists Should Talk with One Another* (Abingdon, 1999) with Henry H. Knight, III; and of *A Song to Sing, a Life to Live:*

Reflections on Music as Spiritual Practice (Wiley, 2006) with his daughter Emily Saliers, a member of the Indigo Girls.

Luther E. Smith Jr. is Professor Emeritus of Church and Community. He is the author of *Howard Thurman: The Mystic as Prophet* (Orbis, 1981) and *Intimacy and Mission: Intentional Community as Crucible for Radical Discipleship* (Wipf & Stock, 1994), and the editor of the *Pan-Methodist Social Witness Resource Book* (African Methodist Episcopal Church Publishing House, 1991) and *Howard Thurman: Essential Writings* (Orbis, 2006). He has written numerous articles and speaks extensively on issues of church and society, congregational renewal, Christian spirituality, and the thought of Howard Thurman.

Smith's current research focuses on the writings and correspondence of Howard Thurman, advocacy on behalf of children, and a spirituality of hope. In 2009 he received the Big Voice for Georgia's Children Award from the group Voices for Georgia's Children, Inc., and the Bishops Thomas Hoyt and Paul Stewart Institutional Ministry Award for Outstanding Service to the Ministry of Academics from the Phillips School of Theology at the Interdenominational Theological Center.

Ted A. Smith is Associate Professor of Preaching and Ethics. He works at the intersections of practical and political theology, tracing connections between everyday church life and basic questions of politics and culture. Prior to coming to Candler, Smith taught at Vanderbilt Divinity School, where he served as director of the Program in Theology and Practice. At Emory, Smith also teaches in the Graduate Division of Religion and is affiliated with the Center for the Study of Law and Religion.

Smith is the author of two books, *The New Measures: A Theological History of Democratic Practice* (Cambridge University Press, 2007) and *Weird John Brown: Divine Violence and the Limits of Ethics* (Stanford University Press, 2014), and has written numerous essays for both scholarly and popular publications. He is the co-editor of *Questions Preachers Ask: Essays in Honor of Thomas G. Long* (Westminster John Knox, 2016) with Scott Black Johnston and Leonora Tubbs Tisdale. He serves on the Board of Directors for the Louisville Institute and on the editorial boards of *Political Theology* and *Practical Matters*. Smith is currently administering a major grant from the

Lilly Foundation for a project on "Theological Education Between the Times," which gathers diverse groups of scholars to think together about the purpose of theological education in a time of great change.

Brent A. Strawn is Professor of Old Testament and director of the Doctor of Ministry program. Before joining the Candler faculty in 2001, he taught at Rutgers University and Asbury Theological Seminary, held a visiting lecturer position at Princeton Theological Seminary, and taught as a visiting professor at Columbia Theological Seminary. He conducts research in ancient Near Eastern iconography, the Dead Sea Scrolls, Israelite religion, legal traditions of the Old Testament, and Old Testament theology. Within the Old Testament proper, he works in the Pentateuch and poetry, focusing especially on Deuteronomy, the Psalms, and theological exegesis.

Strawn has published over two hundred articles, contributions to reference works, and reviews. He is the author of *What Is Stronger than a Lion? Leonine Image and Metaphor in the Hebrew Bible and the Ancient Near East* (Vandenhoeck & Ruprecht, 2005) and *The Old Testament Is Dying: A Diagnosis and Recommended Treatment* (Baker Academic, 2017). Strawn is a prolific editor, editing or coediting twenty volumes to date, including *The Oxford Encyclopedia of the Bible and Law* (Oxford University Press, 2014), for which he served as editor-in-chief; the book received the 2016 Dartmouth Medal for most outstanding reference work. He coedits the *Old Testament Theology* series for Cambridge University Press and sits on the editorial boards of the *Catholic Biblical Quarterly*, the *Journal of Biblical Literature*, the *Old Testament Library*, the series *Explorations in Ancient Near Eastern Culture*, and the series *Interpretation: Resources for the Use of Scripture in the Church*. He also serves on the editorial board of the *Common English Bible* as academic editor and translator. In addition to speaking and preaching regularly at churches across the country, he has also appeared frequently on CNN as a commentator on matters ranging from Easter celebrations to Pope Francis to gun violence.

Steven M. Tipton is Charles Howard Candler Professor Emeritus of Sociology of Religion. After retiring from the faculty in 2016, he was named Senior Research Fellow. In addition to teaching sociology of religion, morality, and culture at Candler since 1979, he has taught related courses in the Department of Sociology and directed Emory's Graduate Division of Religion from 1998 to 2003. In addition to numerous articles, his published works include *Getting Saved from the Sixties: Moral Meaning in Conversion and Cultural Change* (University of California Press, 1982; 2nd ed. Wipf & Stock, 2014), and *Public Pulpits: Methodists and Mainline Churches in the Moral Argument of Public Life* (University of Chicago Press, 2007). He is the coauthor of several important works, including *Habits of the Heart: Individualism and Commitment in American Life* (University of California Press, 1st ed., 1985; 3rd ed., 2008) with Robert N. Bellah et al., and *The Good Society* (Alfred A. Knopf, 1991) with Robert N. Bellah et al. He co-edited *Meaning and Modernity: Religion, Polity and Self* (University of California Press, 2001) with Richard Madsen, et al., and *Family Transformed: Religion, Values, and Society in American Life* (Georgetown University Press, 2007) with John Witte, Jr.

Tipton's current research explores the moral dimensions of American religion, culture, and public institutions in terms that couple interpretive sociology with comparative ethics to shed light on how persons situated in social space and historical time make multi-vocal moral sense of their lives within communities of shared practice and discourse.

CPSIA information can be obtained
at www.ICGtesting.com
Printed in the USA
FSOW01n0145210717
36396FS

9 781945 935039